CONTRA MUNDUM SWAGGER

Contra Mundum Swagger

Following Christ in a Divorce Culture

———

Jack Shannon

Contact the author at
contramundumswagger@gmail.com.

ISBN-13: 9780692838969
ISBN-10: 0692838961

To my father, who taught me what it is to be a prophet, priest, and king.

CONTENTS

GRATITUDE

——

IN HIS COMMENTARY ON ROMANS, John Calvin notes that Paul condemns all mankind from the beginning of the world for its ingratitude. So I figured it wouldn't be a terrible idea to express some gratitude here at the beginning of this book.

First, all thanks and glory be to my God, who is the God of Abraham, Isaac, and Jacob, who sent His Son to die and resurrect and poured out His Spirit for the life of the world. All this belongs to Him and is for His glory.

There have been several pastors in my life, from my childhood to very recently, whom I admire and respect greatly. Out of respect, I won't name them, because I don't want to mislead the reader into thinking they agree with what I have written in this book. They do not and, barring a miracle of God, probably never will. Nevertheless, I am incredibly grateful for the work they have done for the kingdom. Each one has contributed in significant ways and has brought various degrees of purity to the Church. I respect them very much as I have learned different yet important things from all of them. I am grateful for the advancements they have made in the kingdom. I also have several estranged friends whom I respect and have learned much from. Some of them have the deepest hearts and sharpest minds, and I am grateful for the treasured things I learned from them.

I want to thank Dr. David Stehlik for his friendship and wisdom and zeal for the Lord and prayer. I have learned much from him and am indebted to his kindness and patience toward me. I want to thank Kevin Boyle and Mat Szula for their friendship and faithfulness to the word of God. With them

I have experienced what it is to live Psalm 133:1: "Behold, how good and pleasant it is when brothers dwell in unity!" I want to thank my sister, Alyssa Shannon, for exhibiting the glory and boldness of godly femininity, which is rare. This has been an encouragement to me. She has the resolve and adventure of Swede from *Peace like a River* and the fire of Joan of Arc as described by G. K. Chesterton in *Orthodoxy*. I want to thank my brother Dan and his wife, Jena Shannon, for standing for truth and living a faithful marriage in an era when marriage is under attack by those who are supposed to be our allies.

Last, I want to thank my father, Kerry Shannon, for being a great father—not just a physical father but a spiritual one too. In some ways, this book is his, and I feel as if I am merely his mouthpiece. I am simply giving articulation to what he has lived. He is the most humble, courageous, and godly Christian I know. He has shown me what it is to listen to the Holy Spirit and not be afraid of spiritual gifts. He has shown me how to love God's word and to obey it with all my heart. He has shown me what it is to be a warrior and to exercise dominion through the power of righteousness. He saved my life by sacrificing his own. He showed me what it was to be a Christian with the entirety of his life. He is the greatest man I know, and I cannot adequately express the gratitude I have for knowing him.

THE TELOS OF FLAME-THROWING

———

THIS BOOK IS NOT A detailed analysis of every argument for and against what is often called the permanency or traditional position of marriage, divorce, and remarriage. Other men who are more equipped for that task have made compelling arguments elsewhere.[1] Rather, this book essentially assumes the truth of the traditional teachings on marriage and seeks to elaborate what this truth means as it pertains to the individual, the family, the culture, and politics.

Consequently, I present only abbreviated arguments for the doctrine proper in the first two chapters. The traditional doctrine states that while divorce may be permitted in the event of adultery or desertion, any remarriage is adulterous while the former spouse is still living. This is what Jesus and Paul taught, as recorded in Scripture. It was the near-unanimous teaching of the Church in the West for about fifteen hundred years prior to the Reformation, was maintained in various denominations through the twentieth century, and is still practiced in some denominations to this day. However, it is a minority

---

1 Gordon Wenham's *Jesus and Divorce* argues against any exception to divorce and remarriage; however, his application is wrong in that he does not require adulterous marriages to be repented of in any meaningful sense. John Piper, Voddie Baucham, and others have made similar arguments with the same illogical and weak application. The literature from the Protestant Reformed Church is clear and concise, and its application is mostly correct in that it requires those in adulterous marriages to separate or be excommunicated. Craig Keener, William Luck, David Instone-Brewer, John Murray, and many others have written well-researched books on this topic but have argued for various modern interpretations that allow for divorce and remarriage in certain cases.

position within the Church currently—and by *Church* I mean all Christians who confess Jesus as Lord and Savior and have been baptized in the name of the Father, Son, and Holy Spirit.

Chapters 3 and 4 deal with how God views our worship and churches. Chapters 5 through 7 offer a solution to the mess we are in and examples from Scripture to reinforce this proposed solution. Chapter 8 offers a vision of the future that God promises us if we repent and obey.

The purpose of this book is not merely to rebuke the Church of her unrepentant, defiant, and abominable sin of divorce and remarriage but to call her to repentance and restoration. I want to give our leaders and those who are perpetuating this abomination an exhortation to lead us well and to undo their complicity in the fall of the West. I want them to see how this issue is bigger than they are. I want them to see higher and further, and I ultimately want to see them come and fight with me. I would much rather fight with my brothers against Philistines than fight against Benjamin or Ephraim, my brothers. But this book is also a warning to my brother Ephraim, the evangelicals. God is going to stop you from doing what you love to do and is going to put a yoke on your neck: "Ephraim is a trained heifer that loves to thresh; so I will put a yoke on her fair neck. I will drive Ephraim, Judah must plow, and Jacob must break up the ground" (Hosea 10:11). The nature of your work is going to change, so be ready.

The purpose of this book is also to provide encouragement to Christians who feel as if they are alone in following Christ when most of the Church is not following Christ's teachings on marriage. There are thousands of us who have not bowed the knee to Baal. I hope this book will help to articulate some of the things that you perceive with your spirit but haven't been able to express with words. I want you to know that your suffering has meaning beyond yourself. Your cross bearing is purposeful and will not go unrewarded.

Finally, the main purpose of this book is to provide a larger vision of what is happening currently in our churches, in our culture, and in our world and how the Church's teaching and practice on marriage is foundational to our failure and our success. Our teachings on marriage are like Odysseus's bed—carved from a thick olive tree that is growing out of the ground. The rest of Odysseus's house is built around the marriage bed. So it is with marriage and culture. Marriage is foundational, and culture is built around it. The symbolic significance of this is articulated by Paul when he says, "Let marriage be held in honor among all, and let the marriage bed be undefiled, for God will judge the sexually immoral and adulterous" (Hebrews 13:4).

I want to demonstrate that our disobedience on this issue is a fundamental reason for the havoc we are witnessing in our culture and that our obedience to Christ on this issue will also be a fundamental reason for the victory and restoration of our families, churches, culture, and politics. Christ is the ultimate foundation of culture, but from Christ come institutions and commands that serve to either destroy or build, depending on our adherence or disregard.

Our politics, culture, and churches are falling apart, and the root cause of this decay is divorce and remarriage. In this doctrine, all our worst flaws have coalesced. And so it is a bigger problem than adulterous marriages. It reaches down to the foundations of our faith—the lordship of Christ over all things, repentance, obedience, forgiveness, love, and many other foundational issues that the Church has perverted or simply rejected. If we would only repent for our wrong teaching and practice that permits adulterous marriages to be in communion with the body of Christ, these other errors would be exposed more fully, and we would begin to heal our churches, which in turn would heal our culture and, ultimately, our politics.

I don't intend this book to say everything that needs to be said, and I don't pretend to be a man of perfection. I am a sinner turned saint, sanctified daily by the power of the Holy Spirit, striving for perfection, but imperfectly attempting to give medicine to a sick Church that continually misdiagnoses her illness. I do not desire to build myself up by tearing others down. I am not motivated by the guilt of my own sin. I am not bitter toward anyone. My motivation is a deep and sincere love for God's people. These words are written as an act of love and compassion for a sick people. But the Church's sickness is not like the flu or like a cold. It is like rabies. She is sick like a rabid dog and is thrashing about and snarling at anyone who offers genuine help. She refuses to take her medicine. Forgive me if the image of subduing a rabid woman is rough for you. It isn't a pretty picture, and I will probably spill some medicine in the process.

I have sincere love for my brothers and sisters in Christ and true respect for the leadership in the Church, but I also realize that we are in a time when that leadership is failing to protect the sheep. The leaders, along with the people, are too afraid or too deceived to say or do anything about it. It is a strange position to have genuine respect and also genuine revulsion for God's people, but it is not unprecedented. It is something that is everywhere in the Bible, and so I do not consider myself unique in this regard. Consequently, the severity of chastisement in this book is proportionate to the sincerity of love I have for God's people.

In his *Ecclesiastical Laws*, Richard Hooker warns of the radical excess that usually characterizes those who rebuke errors in the Church. He points out the ways in which men attack their superiors and then trace all problems to one doctrine and how this deceptively lends seeming credibility to them and their arguments. Hooker's observations are exact and perceptive. This happens in many situations but not in every situation. Hooker and those sophisticated minds who are more tempered by reasonable dispositions would and will undoubtedly accuse me of being guilty of this type of excess. So be it.

I am not unaware of the tactics radicals use in trying to win people over, but just because excessive radicals employ these tactics doesn't mean they are wrong in every situation. Sometimes the situation, if correctly perceived, requires one to trace most ills to one erroneous doctrine and to attack one's superiors. Otherwise what would we say about all the prophets and apostles in Scripture who did the same? What would we say about Martin Luther? Of the Reformers? There is a time for everything. And the time for denouncing our leadership's position on divorce and remarriage is now, as is the time for recognizing our outstanding failure to win the culture because of our unfaithfulness on this issue.

There are some within the traditionalist camp who are indeed excessive and animated by a fanatical revolutionary spirit. They want to burn everything down and overthrow every ecclesiastical authority. I acknowledge this and lament it. They accurately see the wickedness. They see that the Church has rejected Christ as the Samaritan village did, and like James and John, they want fire to come down from heaven, but they don't know what spirit they are of and ought to be rebuked as well (Luke 9:51–55).

I want to distance myself from these radicals, but I want also to affirm that they are my brothers and sisters, and they put many evangelicals and Reformed Christians to shame with their zeal for holiness and their willingness to follow Christ at any cost.

There will be accusations and condemnations of all types against anyone who speaks against the idolatry of divorce and remarriage in the Church. "In fact, everyone who wants to live a godly life in Christ Jesus will be persecuted" (2 Timothy 3:12). I do not wish to enumerate every type of accusation that typically accompanies those who want to defend this idolatry, and I do not wish to defend myself against every accusation either (though I would be justified in doing so). I do, however, want to address the accusation that will inevitably be made about this book: that the tone is unwarranted.

If I am wrong that divorce and remarriage is adultery, then I agree that my tone is unwarranted. But if divorce and remarriage is adultery, then my tone is absolutely warranted and is arguably more charitable than what is actually warranted. So I want to give a brief defense of the tone before concluding.

Throughout Scripture, the harshest rebukes are often reserved for the leaders of Israel (I will use the terms Israel and *the Church* interchangeably throughout to refer to God's people). When the leaders entrusted with shepherding the people of God egregiously fail, God rebukes them and often does so harshly: "Harsh discipline is for him who forsakes the way, and he who hates correction will die" (Proverbs 15:10).

Conservative Christians tend to be more comfortable with sharp rebuke when it's aimed at nonbelievers, like proponents of homosexuality, or they tend to pick on easy targets like Joel Osteen or a rather obvious heretic. Or they tend to quibble over things like baptism and eschatology, which are important but are not necessarily salvific issues. On the other hand, you have people who are incessantly critical of Church leadership and never want to submit to or honor higher authority. I want to strike a balance (which will inevitably be castigated as an imbalance). I want to be grateful and honorific of the treasures and good things that have been given to us by Church leaders, past and present, but I want to rebuke their folly with pure motives and with the sharpest words possible. Why? Because they deserve both. They deserve honor. Give honor to whom honor is due (Romans 13:7). They also deserve rebuke: "As for those who persist in sin, rebuke them in the presence of all, so that the rest may stand in fear" (1 Timothy 5:20). Love must be sincere by hating what is evil and clinging to what is good (Romans 12:9).

Instead of rebuking the folly of the world, quibbling over tertiary doctrine, or railing against Church leadership for petty things, the Church *must* turn to the issues that are the camels we have swallowed with ease and focus its rebuke on those who are in leadership, whom we may love the most but who have also caused the most damage. I have the utmost respect and truest profound love for many of the men on the wrong side of this issue, and yet that love and respect must never supersede the love and respect I have for Christ. This book is born out of a prioritized love for Christ first and my brothers and sisters in Christ second.

What could be more full of meaning?—for the pulpit is ever this
earth's foremost part; all the rest comes in its rear; the pulpit
leads the world. From thence it is the storm of God's quick
wrath is first descried, and the bow must bear the earliest brunt.
From thence it is the God of breezes fair or foul is first invoked
for favourable winds. Yes, the world's a ship on its passage
out, and not a voyage complete; and the pulpit is its prow.

—HERMAN MELVILLE, *MOBY DICK*, CHAPTER 8, "THE PULPIT"

CHAPTER 1

YOUR CHURCH IS A BROTHEL

———

WHEN YOU GO TO YOUR local church, you're going to a whorehouse. The people you worship with on Sunday morning are in adulterous marriages or are indifferent to the adulterous marriages of the people they worship with. Your pastor and elders may be in unlawful, adulterous marriages. You might even be in one yourself. And while you're amening your pastor's roaring censure of homosexual marriage, you or people nearby are sitting there pretending to be someone else's wife or husband and pretending to be the mother or father of someone else's kids. You're having sex with someone else's spouse, and everyone in the church, including your pastor, allowed this abomination to occur. Your church is a brothel open for business, and business is booming!

Evangelicals don't care much about God's law, it seems, unless it's being removed from the front lawn of a county courthouse. But in those Ten Commandments, we are commanded not to commit adultery. Jesus explains that this means more than just cheating on your spouse or having sex with someone else's spouse. It includes not lusting with your eyes or in your heart for another person's spouse and also not marrying a divorced person whose spouse is still alive and not divorcing and remarrying.

Jesus's teachings on this issue are found in Genesis, in the Gospels of Matthew, Mark, and Luke, and then again in Paul's epistles to the Corinthians and Romans. As I mentioned in the introduction, the arguments fully explaining these passages have been dealt with in much greater detail elsewhere. But I want to put the words of Christ and His Apostle here to provide the foundations of the arguments that are laid out in this book.

Furthermore it has been said, "Whoever divorces his wife, let him give her a certificate of divorce." But I say to you that whoever divorces his wife for any reason except sexual immorality causes her to commit adultery; and whoever marries a woman who is divorced commits adultery. (Matthew 5:31–32)

Jesus is teaching us about the responsibility of the husband who divorces his wife. If he divorces her for sexual immorality, he does not cause her to sin by seeking another man to marry. Even though it would still be objectively sinful for her to marry someone else, the man who divorced her for her sexual immorality isn't culpable for her sexual immorality in this case. But if he divorces her for any reason other than sexual immorality, he causes her to commit sexual immorality, because she will seek to be married to another man. He bears the responsibility of her sin in this case. Essentially, Jesus is saying that the Jews misread the purpose of the divorce certificate. It was permissible for hardness of heart, but it was never intended to allow remarriage. In Deuteronomy 24:1-4, the woman is defiled because of the second marriage. The Jews misread the purpose of this law, and we are doing the same thing now. We justify our remarriages before men because we have a certificate of divorce, but Jesus says it's adultery. In Matthew 5, Jesus is going through the law, explaining how the Jews have misinterpreted it. This section is no different.

The Pharisees also came to Him, testing Him, and saying to Him, "Is it lawful for a man to divorce his wife for just any reason?" And He answered and said to them, "Have you not read that He who made them at the beginning 'made them male and female,' and said, 'For this reason a man shall leave his father and mother and be joined to his wife, and the two shall become one flesh'? So then, they are no longer two but one flesh. Therefore what God has joined together, let not man separate." They said to Him, "Why then did Moses command to give a certificate of divorce, and to put her away?" He said to them, "Moses, because of the hardness of your hearts, permitted you to divorce your wives, but from the beginning it was not so. And I say to you, whoever divorces his wife, except for sexual immorality, and marries another, commits adultery; and whoever marries her who is divorced commits adultery." His disciples said to Him, "If such is the case of the man with his wife, it is better not to marry." But He said to them, "All cannot accept this saying, but only those to whom it has been given: For there are eunuchs who were born thus from their mother's womb, and there are eunuchs who were made eunuchs by men, and there are eunuchs who have made themselves eunuchs for the kingdom of heaven's sake. He who is able to accept it, let him accept it." (Matthew 19:3–12)

This passage is the most quoted passage by divorce-remarriage apologists. Sometimes I think it's the only one they're aware of. They interpret it to mean that Jesus allows remarriage in the case of adultery. But this innovative, modern interpretation is not how virtually anyone in the first fifteen hundred years of the Church in the West understood this verse. It was generally interpreted to allow for divorce in the case of unrepentant adultery but not to allow for remarriage in any case. I believe this is the correct interpretation, as it does justice to harmonizing it with every other text that addresses the issue. Sound hermeneutics demand the passage be interpreted this way. You never interpret clear Scripture with unclear Scripture. The clear Scripture is to interpret the unclear (*Westminster Confession of Faith* 1.9). Matthew 19:9 has approximately eight various interpretations owing to its unclear nature. It would be foolishness to base an entire doctrine on one interpretation of this one verse, which is what the modern Church has done. I will address this more thoroughly in the next chapter. For now, I'll simply say that the weight of history and proper interpretational methods favor the traditional reading.

The Pharisees came and asked Him, "Is it lawful for a man to divorce his wife?" testing Him. And He answered and said to them, "What did Moses command you?" They said, "Moses permitted a man to write a certificate of divorce, and to dismiss her." And Jesus answered and said to them, "Because of the hardness of your heart he wrote you this precept. But from the beginning of the creation, God 'made them male and female.' 'For this reason a man shall leave his father and mother and be joined to his wife, and the two shall become one flesh'; so then they are no longer two, but one flesh. Therefore what God has joined together, let not man separate." In the house His disciples also asked Him again about the same matter. So He said to them, "Whoever divorces his wife and marries another commits adultery against her. And if a woman divorces her husband and marries another, she commits adultery." (Mark 10:2–12)

Now the Pharisees, who were lovers of money, also heard all these things, and they derided Him. And He said to them, "You are those who justify yourselves before men, but God knows your hearts. For what is highly esteemed among men is an abomination in the sight of God. The law and the prophets were until John. Since that time the kingdom of God has been preached, and everyone is pressing into it. And it is easier for heaven and earth to pass away than for one tittle of the law to fail. Everyone who divorces his wife and marries another commits adultery, and he who marries one who is divorced from a husband commits adultery." (Luke 16:14–18)

Christ's teachings in Mark and Luke give total prohibitions of remarriage after divorce. Jesus calls it adultery, and the Greek is in the present indicative, which means continuous adultery, as opposed to being punctiliar, a onetime thing.

Now to the married I command, yet not I but the Lord: A wife is not to depart from her husband. But even if she does depart, let her remain unmarried or be reconciled to her husband. And a husband is not to divorce his wife. (1 Corinthians 7:10–11)

A wife is bound by law as long as her husband lives; but if her husband dies, she is at liberty to be married to whom she wishes, only in the Lord. (1 Corinthians 7:39)

When Paul summarizes Jesus's teachings in 1 Corinthians 7:10–11, he gives no exceptions. When Paul is giving advice outside of the summary of the Lord's teachings, he gives permission for a spouse not to follow a deserting nonbelieving spouse (1 Corinthians 7:15). "Not under bondage" means they are not under any obligation to follow their deserting, unbelieving spouses and that by remaining single and praying for reconciliation, as the Lord commands in such a situation (1 Corinthians 7:11), they may convert their spouses (1 Corinthians 7:16). It is pure eisegesis to assume that Paul is allowing remarriage here, as it contradicts everything Jesus and Paul have said up until this point and elsewhere.

> For the woman who has a husband is bound by the law to her husband as long as he lives. But if the husband dies, she is released from the law of her husband. So then if, while her husband lives, she marries another man, she will be called an adulteress; but if her husband dies, she is free from that law, so that she is no adulteress, though she has married another man. (Romans 7:2–3)

When Paul gives explicit permission for a spouse to marry again, it is only after the death of the spouse, just as our marriage vows state "till death do us part" (see 1 Corinthians 7:39 and Romans 7:2–3). For Paul, an Apostle of Jesus, only death dissolves a marriage covenant. Only death is legitimate grounds for remarriage. Anything beyond this is adultery.

That Scripture teaches that marriage is for life is all very straightforward, but we complicate it because we suppress the truth in our unrighteousness. The simple teaching that marriage is for a lifetime even in the event of divorce is what the Church in the West taught virtually unanimously for fifteen hundred years. The Protestant branch of the Church has been fragmented on this doctrine for the last five hundred years, with some segments maintaining the traditional interpretation and others permitting new interpretations that allow divorce and remarriage in various situations.

According to the National Center for Health Statistics, divorce rates accelerated significantly during the two world wars of the twentieth century, particularly the Second World War.[2] So while the doctrine of permitting

---

2 US Department of Health, Education, and Welfare, "100 Years of Marriage and Divorce Statistics United States 1867--1967" (Rockville, MD: US Department of Health, Education, and Welfare, December 1973). https://www.cdc.gov/nchs/data/series/sr_21/sr21_024.pdf.

remarriage in certain instances began five hundred years ago, it has increased significantly in practice in the past seventy years. The exceptions to divorce and remarriage introduced five hundred years ago were a Trojan horse that brought in the permission for divorce and remarriage in all cases, and have subsequently been the catalyst of the destruction of the family, the Church, culture, and the state. Currently, the evangelical consensus is that divorce and remarriage is permissible in all cases, even if they say they permit it only in certain cases. They pay lip service to the indissolubility of marriage, but they mean that marriage is ideally indissoluble, not that it is indissoluble in reality.

The main issue divorce-remarriage apologists object to with the traditional interpretation is that repentance entails separation. In other words, they are horrified when you suggest that a Christian in sin should not sin. They perform Olympic-level gymnastics, worthy of gold medals, with Scripture to argue that repentance from an adulterous marriage does not mean separation, or they simply resort to weapons-grade personal attacks to discredit the argument. We have no argument here; bring out the ad hominems! Where are my pearls? For I must clutch them! This horror and defensiveness reveals where their faithfulness lies. Follow Christ at all costs, or defend my little kingdom at all costs?

I bring this up because the reactions I have encountered against what I am suggesting are not warranted, as this mode of repentance has the support of Scripture and the weight of history on its side. If divorce and remarriage is continuous adultery, then the obvious conclusion is that those in that sin need to repent by separating themselves from it. The proper application, needing to repent via separation, is avoided by some (not all) of the best modern scholars who defend the traditional interpretation—but it was not avoided by the scholars of the past. Not every quotation that follows addresses the application of the traditional interpretation, but some of them do.

THE DEMOCRACY OF THE DEAD

Many Christians have told me on several occasions that nobody believes that divorce and remarriage is adultery or that those who do don't believe it is *continuous* adultery, which means they don't need to change their lives, which means basically nothing. How surprising! The Church is advocating another impotent doctrine out of shameless self-preservation. I have been met with condescending derision by Christians who say that the traditional doctrine is fanatical and heterodox.

These types of assertions come from desperation. The defenders of divorce and remarriage are obligated to minimize the traditional doctrine, even out of virtually complete ignorance, in order to preserve their social lives. Throughout history, the Christian Church in the West has proven their assertions to be wrong. Some of the West's theological giants, like Jerome, Augustine, and Aquinas, and many Church councils, all believed that Scripture taught traditional marriage (that divorce and remarriage is adultery and that those who desire to repent must separate from their adulterous unions). The following is an abbreviated survey of the Western Church's thoughts on this doctrine for the past two thousand years:

The Shepherd of Hermas (c. AD 90):

And I said to him, "What then, sir, is the husband to do, if his wife continue in her vicious practices?" And he said, "The husband should put her away, and remain by himself. But if he put his wife away and marry another, he also commits adultery."[3]

Justin Martyr (c. AD 150):

"Whosoever shall marry her that is divorced from another husband, commits adultery." So that all who, by human law, are twice married, are in the eye of our Master sinners, and those who look upon a woman to lust after her.[4]

---

3 "Commandment 4, Chapter One," from *Ante-Nicene Fathers Volume 1: The Shepherd of Hermas, Book II*, trans. F. Crombie, ed. Alexander Roberts, James Donaldson, and A. Cleveland Coxe (Buffalo, NY: Christian Literature Publishing Co., 1885). Revised and edited for New Advent by Kevin Knight. http://www.newadvent.org/fathers/02012.htm.

4 "Chapter Fifteen" from *Ante-Nicene Fathers, Volume 1: First Apology of Justin Martyr*, trans. Marcus Dods and George Reith, ed. Alexander Roberts, James Donaldson, and A. Cleveland Coxe (Buffalo, NY: Christian Literature Publishing Co., 1885). Revised and edited for New Advent by Kevin Knight. http://www.newadvent.org/fathers/0126.htm.

Clement of Alexandria (c. AD 208):

"He that takes a woman that has been put away," it is said, "commits adultery; and if one puts away his wife, he makes her an adulteress," that is, compels her to commit adultery. And not only is he who puts her away guilty of this, but he who takes her, by giving to the woman the opportunity of sinning; for did he not take her, she would return to her husband.[5]

Council of Arles, canon 10 (c. AD 314):

Of those who discover their wives in adultery and are young Christians and are forbidden to marry, it was determined that they be most strongly advised not to take other wives while their own live, though they be adulterous.[6]

Council of Elvira (c. AD 324):

A Christian woman who has left an adulterous Christian husband and is marrying another is to be forbidden to marry; if, however, she has already remarried, she is not to receive communion before the death of the man whom she has left, unless mortal sickness compels it.[7]

Jerome (c. AD 396):

Therefore if your sister, who, as she says, has been forced into a second union, wishes to receive the body of Christ and not to be

---

5 "Chapter Twenty-Three: On Marriage," from *Ante-Nicene Fathers, Volume 2: The Stromata, Book II*, trans. William Wilson, ed. Alexander Roberts, James Donaldson, and A. Cleveland Coxe (Buffalo, NY: Christian Literature Publishing Co., 1885) Revised and edited for New Advent by Kevin Knight. http://www.newadvent.org/fathers/02102.htm.

6 "Divorce," *The Church Quarterly Review*, Vol. XL, No. LXXIX (1895): 21.

7 Ibid., 21.

accounted an adulteress, let her do penance; so far at least as from
the time she begins to repent to have no farther intercourse with
that second husband who ought to be called not a husband but an
adulterer.[8]

Apostolic Canon 48 (c. AD 400):

If a layman divorces his own wife, and takes another, or one divorced
by another, let him be excommunicated.[9]

Augustine (c. AD 401):

Seeing that the compact of marriage is not done away by divorce
intervening; so that they continue wedded persons one to another,
even after separation; and commit adultery with those, with whom
they shall be joined, even after their own divorce, either the woman
with a man, or the man with a woman.[10]

Innocent I (c. AD 402–17):

It is manifest that when persons who have been divorced marry
again both parties are adulterers. And moreover, although the

---

8 "Jerome Letter 55 to Amandus, Section 3," from *Nicene and Post-Nicene Fathers, Second Series, Volume 6*, trans. W. H. Fremantle, G. Lewis, and W. G. Martley, ed. Philip Schaff and Henry Wace (Buffalo, NY: Christian Literature Publishing Co., 1893). Revised and edited for New Advent by Kevin Knight. http://www.newadvent.org/fathers/3001055.htm.

9 *Nicene and Post-Nicene Fathers, Second Series, Volume 14*, trans. Henry Percival, ed. Philip Schaff and Henry Wace (Buffalo, NY: Christian Literature Publishing Co., 1900). Revised and edited for New Advent by Kevin Knight. http://www.newadvent.org/fathers/3820.htm.

10 "Sections 6–7 On the Good of Marriage," from *Nicene and Post-Nicene Fathers, First Series, Volume 3*, trans. C. L. Cornish, ed. Philip Schaff (Buffalo, NY: Christian Literature Publishing Co., 1887). Revised and edited for New Advent by Kevin Knight. http://www.newadvent.org/fathers/1309.htm.

former marriage is supposed to be broken, yet if they marry again they themselves are adulterers, but the parties whom they marry are equally with them guilty of adultery; as we read in the gospel: "He who puts away his wife and marries another commits adultery"; and likewise, "He who marries her that is put away from her husband commits adultery." Therefore all such are to be repelled from communion.[11]

Council of Carthage, canon 102 (c. AD 418):

It seemed good that according to evangelical and discipline a man who had been put away from his wife, and a woman put away from her husband should not be married to another, but so should remain, or else be reconciled the one to the other.[12]

Finnian of Clonard (c. AD 550):

We declare against separating a wife from her husband; but if she has left him, [we declare] that she remain unmarried or be reconciled to her husband according to the Apostle. If a man's wife commits fornication and cohabits with another man, he ought not to take another wife while his wife is alive... So also a woman, if she has been sent away by her husband, must not mate with another man so long as her former husband is in the body; but she should wait for him, unmarried, in all patient chastity, in the hope that God may perchance put patience in the heart of her husband.[13]

---

11 *Innocentius, Papa.* Epist. III. ad I. Exuperium, cap 6. Cited in John Fulton, *The Laws of Marriage* (New York, NY: E. & J. B. Young, 1883), 255.

12 *Nicene and Post-Nicene Fathers, Second Series, Volume 14*, trans. Henry Percival, ed. Philip Schaff and Henry Wace (Buffalo, NY: Christian Literature Publishing Co., 1900). Revised and edited for New Advent by Kevin Knight. http://www.newadvent.org/fathers/3816.htm.

13 John T. McNeill and Helena M. Gamer, *Medieval Handbooks of Penance: A Translation of the Principal Libri Poenitentiales and Selections from Related Documents* (New York: Columbia

Council of Nantes, canon 12 (c. AD 658):

> If a man's wife has committed adultery…let him send away his wife, if he will…but her husband may not on any account take another wife while she lives.[14]

The Venerable Bede (c. AD 672–735):

> Therefore is there only one carnal cause, fornication: one spiritual cause, the fear of God for which a wife may be dismissed. But there is no cause prescribed by the law of God that another wife may be taken, while she is alive who has been abandoned.[15]

Council of Friuli, canon 10 (AD 791):

> Though the bond of marriage be broken for the cause of immorality, a man may not marry another wife as long as the adulteress lives, though she be an adulteress; and the adulteress shall never marry another husband.[16]

Sixth Council of Paris, canon 2 (AD 829):

> And those who marry other wives when their own have been sent away for the cause of immorality are to be marked as adulterers by the judgment of the Lord.[17]

University Press, 1938, 1990), 95.

14 "Divorce," *The Church Quarterly Review*, Vol. XL, No. LXXIX (1895), 18.

15 Henry John Wilkins, *The History of Divorce and Re-Marriage for English Churchmen* (London: Longmans, Green & Co., 1910), 124.

16 "Divorce," *The Church Quarterly Review*, Vol. XL, No. LXXIX (1895), 17.

17 Ibid., 18.

Canon List of Benedict the Levite (c. AD 847):

> That during the lifetime of husband or wife neither of them be united in another marriage…and if she has committed fornication, and her husband desires it, she is to be dismissed, but another wife may not be taken in marriage during her lifetime, because adulterers will not possess the kingdom of God, and her penitence is to be accepted.[18]

Archbishop Dunstan's Penitential Canons of Confession (AD 963):

> He that relinquisheth his Wife, and taketh another Woman breaketh Wedlock. Let none of those Rights which belong to Christians be allowed him, either during Life, or at his Death, nor let him be buried with Christian Men: and let the same be done to a [delinquent] Wife: And let the Kindred that were present at the Contract suffer the same Doom, except they will first be converted, and earnestly make Satisfaction.[19]

Council of Rheims, canon 12 (AD 1049):

> [We decree] that no one, having left his lawful wife, may take another.[20]

Peter Lombard (AD 1100–1164):

> The marriage bond still exists between those who, even if departing from one another, having joined themselves to others.[21]

---

18 Oscar Daniel Watkins, *Holy Matrimony* (London: Rivington, Percival, 1895), 391.

19 Henry John Wilkins, *The History of Divorce and Re-Marriage for English Churchmen* (London: Longmans, Green & Co., 1910), 124.

20 Ibid., 109.

21 Ibid., 111.

Thomas Aquinas (AD 1225–74):

> Nothing supervenient to marriage can dissolve it: wherefore adultery does not make a marriage cease to be valid.[22]

John Wycliffe (AD 1328–84):

> And let each man be aware that he procures no false divorce, for money, neither for friendship, neither for enemy; for Christ commands that no man separate them that God has joined; but only for adultery that party that keeps himself clean may depart from the other's bed and for no other cause, as Christ himself says. And in this case the clean party has the option to either live chastely for as long as the other lives, or else be reconciled again to the other party.[23]

I am not arguing that every person in the West taught or practiced the indissolubility of marriage. There were dissenters and differences and variations for the first fifteen hundred years, especially in the civil realm.[24] But there was certainly a general consensus, especially in the Church.

David Instone-Brewer, a divorce-remarriage apologist, admits this is the case in Church history up until the Reformation: "The general consensus is that marriage is indissoluble except by death, though husband and wife can

---

22 *The Summa Theologiæ of St. Thomas Aquinas, Second and Revised Edition*, 1920, trans. Fathers of the English Dominican Province, online edition, © 2016 by Kevin Knight. http://www.newadvent.org/summa/5062.htm.

23 Thomas Arnold, ed., *Select English Works of John Wycliffe, Volume 3: Miscellaneous* Works (Oxford: Clarendon Press, 1871), 192.

24 David Instone-Brewer, *Divorce and Remarriage in the Bible: The Social and Literary Context* (Cambridge: Wm. B. Eerdmans Publishing Co., 2002), 238-259. This section does not survey civil laws, which tended to be much more relaxed, but it does survey some of the dissenting voices and variations among the Church fathers. See John Milton's "The Judgment of Martin Bucer Concerning Divorce" for examples of permissive civil law regarding divorce and remarriage.

separate 'from bed and hearth' if either commits adultery."[25] He recognizes this to be the traditional view. "The traditional view is that Jesus forbade all divorce except in the case of adultery, and that he forbade all remarriage. This view can be traced through the Church Fathers, Church canon law, and the writings of the Reformers."[26]

I don't know of any Continental Reformer or Puritan who held to the traditional position. In fact, it was the Reformers who introduced on a significant scale the idea that the marriage covenant was dissoluble. I don't know why Instone-Brewer lumped the Reformers in with the traditional interpretation, but it is also possible that I simply haven't read the works of Reformers who held to the traditional interpretation. I highly doubt this is case. Every prominent Reformer and most of their theological progeny I have read held to some form of the dissolubility of the marriage covenant with the exception of the Anglican Church. Thomas Cranmer and William Tyndale both believed in permissible cases for divorce and remarriage, but their views were never instituted due to opposition in King Edward's reign and the conservatism of Queen Elizabeth's.[27]

Erasmus, Luther, and Calvin all argued in favor of limited exceptions that allowed Christians to forsake their vows, such as divorcing for adultery and desertion. Some men, like John Milton and Martin Bucer, argued for exceedingly liberal interpretations, such as permitting divorce and remarriage as long as it was consensual.[28] However, the *Westminster Confession of Faith* statement became the generally accepted position in some Reformed traditions. This stated that a person may divorce in the case of adultery and remarry as if the offending party were dead and that the desertion of an unbelieving spouse is sufficient for dissolving the bond of marriage. This is still the stated position in some confessionally Reformed denominations, but in reality, I've seen them

---

25 David Instone-Brewer, *Divorce and Remarriage in the Bible: The Social and Literary Context* (Cambridge: Wm. B. Eerdmans Publishing Co., 2002), 258.

26 Ibid., 238.

27 Ibid., 263.

28 John Milton, "The Judgment of Martin Bucer Concerning Divorce." https://www.dartmouth.edu/~milton/reading_room/bucer/text.shtml.

permit divorce and remarriage for reasons other than the ones listed in the *Westminster Confession of Faith.*

John Owen mentions that there are other people in his time who maintained traditional views on marriage.[29]

The Anglican Church eventually parted with two millennia of traditional teaching on marriage and divorce at the General Synod of 2002.[30]

The Roman Catholic Church reaffirmed the traditional teaching at the Council of Trent and has maintained the traditional teaching up until the present but, within the past few years, has undergone internal struggle to adopt the modern view (see the disputes between Cardinal Burke and Pope Francis and the concerns raised by the *Amoris Laetitia,* which suggests that those who are divorced and remarried may receive communion).

The Protestant Reformed Church is a Presbyterian denomination that teaches and practices the traditional and biblical position on divorce and remarriage. Several Protestant denominations, such as the Assemblies of God, recovered and then dispensed with the traditional teachings throughout the twentieth century.[31] In addition, other denominations and independent congregations also hold to the biblical teaching on divorce and remarriage, but they are certainly in the minority in this sliver of history. The modern interpretation is certainly favored by the arrogant oligarchy of those who happen to be walking about, to borrow a phrase from G. K. Chesterton.

Looking at the history of thought on this issue helps to triangulate where we currently are and the forces that are at work in our thinking on the subject. Instone-Brewer argues that the Patristics had "little incentive to seek

---

29 John Owen, *The Works of John Owen, Volume 16* (Carlisle: Banner of Truth, 1991), 254–57.

30 Ann Sumner Holmes, "Divorce and Remarriage in the Church of England, 1936-2005: A Comparison of Edward VIII and Prince Charles." *International Journal of the Humanities*, Volume 3, Issue 8, 139-146.

31 For a helpful survey of the history of thought on divorce and remarriage, see "The History of Christian Thought upon Marriage, Divorce & Remarriage" by Daniel Jennings. http://www.danielrjennings.org/ThisHistoryOfChristianThoughtOnMarriageDivorceAndRemarriage.pdf.

ways to help divorcées remarry."[32] One wonders what incentives pastors and theologians currently have for seeking ways to help divorcées remarry. Using Instone-Brewer's logic, we find that he and every other pastor and theologian have overwhelming incentive to argue in favor of divorce and remarriage. They have nothing to lose by arguing in favor of divorce and remarriage and have almost everything to lose by arguing against it.

Gordon Wenham makes a similar point about William Heth in *Remarriage after Divorce in Today's Church: 3 Views*. Wenham coauthored *Jesus and Divorce* with Heth. Heth did most of the work and eventually repudiated his work and changed his mind on divorce and remarriage. Wenham addresses this situation and laments the fact that he has to oppose his colleague in public:

> I am sorry to be in this situation, but I appreciate that the atmosphere in America on this issue is somewhat different from the atmosphere in the United Kingdom, where many in the mainline churches have resisted the idea that the New Testament permits remarriage after divorce. Thus, it is easier for me in the UK to stick my neck out on this matter than it is for an American...all of us in Western society have friends or relatives who have become divorced and have remarried. We know how they suffered in their first marriage, and now they have married again and have found a happiness they did not know in their first marriage; who are we to say that they are wrong and that God disapproves of their present arrangement?[33]

The pressure is high for pastors and theologians to find loopholes that permit divorce and remarriage. This ought to be seriously considered when working through this issue, both by the layperson who is seeking truth and by the pastor/theologian who is teaching it.

---

32 David Instone-Brewer, *Divorce and Remarriage in the Bible: The Social and Literary Context* (Cambridge: Wm. B. Eerdmans Publishing Co., 2002), 257.

33 Gordon Wenham, William Heth, and Craig Keener, *Remarriage after Divorce in Today's Church*, ed. Mark Straus (Grand Rapids: Zondervan, 2006), 85.

I want to conclude by defending the history of thought on this subject generally and the Patristics particularly. The Patristics are often dismissed by moderns because they were ostensibly more ascetic and their theologies weren't as developed or sophisticated as ours are now or because we think that because they didn't know Hebrew and Jewish history well enough, they simply missed some things. There is a lot of truth in some of this, but it is not all true, and it doesn't mean that we have nothing to learn from them. We can look back on the Patristics with chronological snobbery and dismiss them as if they had nothing of value to contribute because their incentives were different or they had ascetic tendencies, but these may also be reasons to hear them out, as our own tendencies and incentives skew our own thinking. It should be realized that where we can easily see their blind spots, they can easily see ours. C. S. Lewis states it well when he says,

> Every age has its own outlook. It is specially good at seeing certain truths and specially liable to make certain mistakes. We all, therefore, need the books that will correct the characteristic mistakes of our own period. And that means the old books. All contemporary writers share to some extent the contemporary outlook—even those, like myself, who seem most opposed to it…we may be sure that the characteristic blindness of the twentieth century—the blindness about which posterity will ask, "But how could they have thought that?"—lies where we have never suspected it.[34]

The outlook of the Church in late antiquity and the medieval ages ought to be seriously regarded in this matter. To invoke G. K. Chesterton's democracy of the dead would only favor the traditional position. But a democratic vote of all the saints in Church history, even if in favor of a permanency view, does not prove it is what Jesus and Paul taught. It is certainly possible that the majority opinion throughout an overwhelming percentage of Church history in the West, beginning immediately with those who lived at the same time as

---

34 C. S. Lewis, introduction to *St. Athanasius on the Incarnation: The Treatise De incarnatione Verbi Dei* (Crestwood: St. Vladimir's Seminary Press, 1993), 4–5.

the apostles, has been unfaithful to what the Scriptures truly teach. This is a possibility, but an unlikely one. At the very least, it must be admitted that the current evangelical consensus on divorce and remarriage is a theological innovation. Whether it's true can be debated, but what can't be debated is that it is a modern view.

The current evangelical consensus is a minority position and a theological novum when considering all Church history in the West. This fact is not immaterial. One must assume and prove that from the first century and in the twenty centuries following, significant Church leaders, theologians, and entire denominations have misunderstood Jesus and Paul. The burden of proof is then on the divorce-remarriage apologists to defend their theological innovation. They must prove the minority position by overthrowing the traditional view of marriage, a biblically and historically rooted consensus, and the majority position. This is a colossal task and one that I'm not convinced anyone has done or can do.

CHAPTER 2

THE DEVIL IS IN THE DOCTRINE

———

I HAVE WRESTLED WITH THE doctrine of divorce and remarriage for about a decade. Over this time, I have spoken with dozens of pastors, read countless position papers, doctrinal statements, and books, and have heard passionate objections from strangers, acquaintances, friends, and family. I've yet to be convinced that the traditional teachings on marriage should be replaced with the modern, innovative ones.

The following addresses some of the more common objections to the traditional view of marriage I've encountered. Some of them are weak, while others are more reasonable but still wrong. This isn't exhaustive, but I hope it's helpful to the sincere seeker of the truth.

GUYS, I FOUND A LOOPHOLE! I WAS WORRIED I MIGHT HAVE TO PICK UP A CROSS...

The exception clause in Matthew 19:9 is the one verse that amateur divorce-remarriage apologists know, if they know any at all. They argue that Jesus allows someone to divorce *and* remarry if a spouse commits adultery. Here are some of the main problems with that reading.

Allowing for remarriage violates sound hermeneutics. Bernard Ramm, in *Protestant Biblical Interpretations*, says, "The obscure passage must yield to the clear passage. That is, on a given doctrine we should take our primary guidance from those passages which are clear rather from those which are obscure.

No Scripture is to be interpreted so as to conflict with any other—the harmony of revelation."[35]

When addressing this specific passage, Augustine says,

> So, because we may not say that when the evangelists use different words to speak about the same matter, they disagree in their understanding of the same doctrine, the only alternative is to understand that Matthew intended the part to stand for the whole,. The view he held, however, was the same…everyone who divorces his wife and marries again is guilty of adultery.[36]

This passage is from an entire treatise Augustine wrote about adulterous marriages. He argued that in order to harmonize all the teachings on divorce and remarriage, one must permit marriage to another only after the spouse has died, and there are no exceptions to this. There are exceptions to divorce, such as infidelity and desertion, but these exceptions do not permit remarriage. He comes to this conclusion by having the obscure passage yield to the clear passages.

The *Westminster Confession of Faith* 1.9 states the same:

> The infallible rule of interpretation of Scripture, is the Scripture itself; and therefore, when there is a question about the true and full sense of any scripture (which is not manifold, but one), it may be searched and known by other places that speak more clearly.

The clear teachings on divorce and remarriage (Matthew 5, Mark 10, Luke 16, 1 Corinthians 7, and Romans 7) prohibit divorce and remarriage in all situations and define subsequent marriages as adultery when the former spouse is

---

35 Bernard Ramm, *Protestant Biblical Interpretation* (Grand Rapids: Baker Books, 1970), 37.
36 Augustine, *Marriage and Virginity: The Excellence of Marriage, Holy Virginity, The Excellence of Widowhood, Adulterous Marriages, Continence.*, trans. Ray Kearney (Hyde Park: New City Press, 1999), 150.

still alive. When Paul summarizes Jesus's teachings in 1 Corinthians 7:10–11, he mentions no exception for sexual immorality. And when Paul grants permission for a previously married person to marry someone else, it is only in the context of the death of the spouse (1 Corinthians 7:39 and Romans 7:2–3). The unclear Scripture of Matthew 19:9 must yield to the clear Scriptures listed above. The modern interpretation forces all these clear Scriptures to yield to Matthew 19:9, which is simply bad hermeneutics.

One may object by saying that Matthew 19 is the clear text, since it is the most extensive passage and provides the most information. One may say that it actually clarifies the other texts, and so it is necessary to harmonize the texts by importing the one exception into every other passage that omits it. The problem is that unlike the clear passages, where the meaning of the text is not disputed, the meaning of Matthew 19:9 has up to eight interpretations, and only two of these allow for remarriage after divorce.

The first seven different interpretations are each explained in Gordon Wenham's *Jesus and Divorce*. If you're interested in exploring these further, then you can reference that book. I will summarize the various interpretations here.

1. The Patristic (or traditional) view—One may divorce in cases of sexual immorality (especially unrepentant sexual immorality) but cannot remarry.
2. The Erasmian view—One may divorce for adultery and remarry.
3. The unlawful marriage view—One may divorce if the marriage itself is incestuous, or even if it is a marriage to a gentile, and is able to remarry.
4. The betrothal view—One may divorce for sexual immorality during the betrothal period and remarry.
5. The preterative view—Jesus is basically saying "no comment." The exception is Jesus's way of bypassing the Pharisaical dispute brought to Him. He isn't taking it into consideration.
6. The inclusive view—The exception clause should be interpreted "not even in the case of adultery."

7. The traditio-historic view—Matthew added the exception. This view doesn't give any new exegetical options (it really isn't another view); it just attempts to understand the text without assuming it harmonizes with other texts.
8. The Matthean harmonization view—Matthew 19:9 is an abbreviated version of Matthew 5:32, which addresses the culpability of the husband in causing his wife to commit sexual immorality.

The other passages, for the most part, do not have this much variation in interpretation. It is generally agreed that the other passages give absolute prohibitions. So it's difficult to argue that this passage is the clear one. And since it is not, we should maintain hermeneutical integrity by interpreting this unclear passage so that it does not contradict the clear passages. If we do this, we find that the traditional view gives the most satisfying interpretation.

Allowing for remarriage makes the surrounding context incoherent. Jesus makes an absolute prohibition when appealing to the creational order in Matthew 19:4–6. This shocks the Pharisees, who don't understand why Moses allowed Israel to divorce. Jesus says Moses allowed it because they were evil men who had hard hearts. According to the trendy, modern views that allow for remarriage, Jesus then walks back His absolute prohibition by allowing for remarriage in the case of adultery. This disrupts the flow of Jesus's argumentation and how He argues in Mark 10. The disciples are shocked and behave as if they had never heard Jesus's teaching before. But according to the modern view, Jesus is teaching the same thing as the Shammai school of Pharisees, who taught that one may divorce and remarry in the event of adultery. So why are the disciples surprised? Why do they act as if Jesus were teaching something they had never heard before? Their surprise does not fit well with the modern interpretation, but it is contextually coherent with the traditional interpretation.

Jesus goes even further by defending celibacy, which would have been against the cultural norms of the Jews, who put a premium on "being fruitful and multiplying," which they understood only in a physical sense. The trajectory of Jesus's argument goes from no divorce and remarriage to no marriage at all if one can accept it. His teachings here go against the Pharisees' pre-suppositions and interpretations at every turn, unless you believe that Jesus allowed for remarriage in the case of adultery. If you believe this to be the case, then you make the context of Matthew 19 incoherent. I have yet to hear a good explanation from the divorce-remarriage apologists who attempt to explain the larger context in this passage.

Certain divorce-remarriage apologists realize that Jesus's response merits the conclusion that He transcends the Pharisees' teachings in *some* way. So they argue that Jesus's position is stricter than the Shammaite view because He allowed for the *option* of divorcing the spouse instead of making it obliga-tory.[37] This still does not explain why there is such a strong response from the disciples. If Jesus is only slightly modifying the Shammaite view, then the disciples' strong reaction is still enigmatic. It also doesn't seem like a stricter position to make divorce optional rather than mandatory.

The context is incoherent if a modern interpretation is to be accepted. But the traditional view makes for coherent contextual understanding, as it gives authority to the created order as opposed to credence to Moses's concession, just as Jesus did, and it also makes the responses of both the Pharisees and Jesus's disciples understandable.

Allowing for remarriage deviates from what the majority of Christians in the West have believed. As surveyed in the previous chapter, the earliest Christians believed that they could divorce for reason of sexual immorality but that they had to remain single or be reconciled. The earliest Christians spoke Greek and understood the nuances of the language better than we do, and none of them believed that adultery was grounds for divorce and remarriage. This was the general doctrine in the Western Church for fifteen hundred years. Have we come into a more biblical understanding? I'm not convinced we have. I believe we have jettisoned the correct biblical understanding.

Those who allow for remarriage in certain cases do not consistently apply their own standards. Those who claim to believe in the exception clauses do not consistently apply them in practice. They say that the innocent spouse

---

37 *English Standard Version Study Bible* (Wheaton: Crossway, 2008), notes on Matthew 19:9.

can remarry. Can the guilty spouse? Why? What about those who remarry but whose divorces were for reasons other than adultery or desertion? Do they need to separate since their marriages are adulterous according to their own standard? They don't? Why not? Every single church I have interacted with and observed on this issue does not consistently apply its own standards. These churches do not require those who are living in adulterous marriages—according to their own standards—to repent via separation. I don't know of anyone who consistently applies these principles, particularly the Reformed churches that subscribe to the *Westminster Confession of Faith.*

I am absolutely convinced that the exception clauses are brought up entirely as a smoke screen. Nobody who argues for these exceptions will say that those who remarry unlawfully, according to their own standards, will make any effort to call the Christians in those unlawful marriages to repentance. They will apply the most illogical, anemic, impotent call to repentance. They will say that the only thing necessary for repentance is that they need to tell God, "Oops! Sorry, God." And then they can stay in their unlawful marriages because God waves a magic wand that makes adulterous marriage not adulterous.

Could the same be applied to homosexual marriages? Of course not. They wouldn't even entertain the idea of saying people in homosexual marriages need to repent by simply asking forgiveness for the unlawful act of marriage or that they need to stay married because God hates divorce and two wrongs don't make a right. What garbage. But they may object that a homosexual marriage is not really a marriage, to which one can reply that a divorce and remarriage is not a marriage either. It's adultery. The exception clauses are the pretense for allowing divorce and remarriage in all cases, which is evidenced in the inconsistent application of the modern interpretations.

Allowing for remarriage after divorce does not comport with God's dealings with Israel. When God divorces Israel in Jeremiah 3, He divorces her for her unrepentant sexual immorality, but He desires for her to return. After giving her a certificate of divorce, He says, "Return, O backsliding children…for I am married to you" (Jeremiah 3:14). According to the modern interpretation, adultery dissolves the marriage covenant like Alka-Seltzer in water. If divorce dissolves the marriage covenant, then how can the Lord tell Israel He is married to her after she commits adultery and He gives her a certificate of divorce? What is going on? Someone needs to explain to God that adultery dissolves the marriage covenant. Perhaps your local pastor or Gospel Coalition blogger wouldn't mind informing God how this whole covenant thing works.

The early Church interpreted Matthew 19:9 to mean ongoing unrepentant, sexual immorality. This is precisely why God divorces Israel, but He does not look for another bride. His desire is for her to return, because despite the certificate of divorce, God still declares that they are married.

This fits with the way in which unrepentant sin is dealt with elsewhere in Scripture. It's really the same model for how to deal with unrepentant sin in the Church. It's a form of excommunication. If someone is in unrepentant sin, it is lawful to excommunicate that person, which is a type of divorce from the body of Christ. But the desire is for these people to repent and return to their covenantal obligations in Christ. Their sin doesn't dissolve the covenant they entered into at baptism, though it may separate them for a time. While they are separated through excommunication (or divorce, by analogy), they are still obligated by the covenant to repent and return to the body of Christ, just as an unfaithful spouse is still obligated to repent and return to their one-flesh body. And the faithful spouse is to model Christ by waiting for the other to return, like the father waiting for his prodigal son.

Moses, in Whom You Trust

When the Pharisees ask Jesus about divorce and remarriage, they want Jesus to comment on Deuteronomy 24:1. Instead, Jesus brings up the creational ordinance in Genesis. The Pharisees are confused and ask why Moses allowed Israelites to divorce their spouses. Jesus says Moses "suffered" them to divorce because of the hardness of their hearts.

Amazingly, I have encountered Reformed Christian pastors who believe hardness of heart is a legitimate reason to divorce and remarry. Never mind that hardness of heart is not listed among their confessional standards as a biblical reason. The *Westminster Confession of Faith* never mentions hardness of heart as grounds for divorce and remarriage. The irony is that Christian leaders make the exact objections that the Pharisees made against Jesus. At some point, your pastor will inevitably say, "But…but Moses!"

And you can say, "If you believed Moses, then you would believe Jesus."

Jesus says, "Do not think that I shall accuse you to the Father; there is one who accuses you—Moses, in whom you trust. For if you believed Moses, you would believe Me; for he wrote about Me. But if you do not believe his writings, how will you believe My words?" (John 5:45–47).

The adulterous-marriage apologists argue that because Deuteronomic law prohibits the return of a divorced and remarried wife to her original husband, it therefore means that the second marriage is legitimate. But the problem with this argument is that the text strongly indicates that the second marriage is adulterous: "Her former husband who divorced her must not take her back to be his wife after she has been defiled; for that is an abomination before the Lord, and you shall not bring sin on the land which the Lord your God is giving you as an inheritance" (Deuteronomy 24:4). The adulterous-marriage apologists emphasize that for her to return to her original husband is considered an abomination. I don't disagree with this. It is an abomination. But what they fail to account for is that the law also says that being divorced and marrying someone else defiles a person.

Peter Craigie, in his commentary on Deuteronomy, says, "The language (defiled) suggests adultery (see Lev. 18:20). The sense is that the woman's remarriage after the first divorce is similar to adultery in that the woman cohabits with another man."[38] So to say that this law justifies divorce and remarriage ignores this fact or comes up with a fanciful explanation as to why the woman has been defiled, but the most natural reading is that the second marriage defiles her.

Additionally, since the Authorized Version translation of Deuteronomy 24:1-4 produced more confusion than clarity, it needs to be noted that the only command in Deuteronomy 24:1–4 is in verse 4. The only legislative element is the prohibition of return. Everything else is descriptive. Moses is

---

38 Peter C. Craigie, *The Book of Deuteronomy* (Grand Rapids: Wm. B. Eerdmans Publishing Co., 1976), 305.

saying, "If this happens, then the woman cannot return to her first husband." Think of Deuteronomy 24:1–4 as an if-then statement. The "if" part is verses 1–3. The "then" part is verse 4. These are the protasis and the apodosis in a conditional sentence. John Calvin interprets it this way, and the Septuagint adopts this construction.[39] Also, "modern scholars...of various theological viewpoints are insistent that the protasis in this passage embraces the first three verses and that it is only at the beginning of verse 4 that the apodosis is introduced."[40]

With this in mind, it is clear that the purpose of the law was not to give men a reason to divorce their wives. It was to discourage remarriage after divorce. As usual, the Pharisees didn't understand the fullness of the law, just like our preachers and theologians today. Jesus provides commentary on this law in Matthew 19 and Mark 10 and clears things up with the Pharisees by telling them that divorcing and remarrying is committing adultery. He does the same thing in the Sermon on the Mount in Matthew 5. He tells them that divorcing a woman does not justify her remarriage; rather, by divorcing a woman, you cause her to commit adultery by remarrying, unless she has already committed adultery. Jesus never says that adultery allows someone to remarry.

In the debate on divorce, I've observed an undue emphasis on the Old Testament, particularly in Reformed circles. This emphasis places the Old Testament in the driver's seat and puts the New Testament in the passenger seat. But the New Testament is to be the driver of the hermeneutical bus. To switch metaphors, the New Testament is the hermeneutical lens by which we interpret the Old Testament. Neglecting to let Jesus interpret the Old Testament is another criticism I would make of the arguments of those who support adulterous modern marriage. They interpret the New Testament by the Old Testament instead of letting the New inform the Old. Tony Sargent's description of Martyn Lloyd-Jones's hermeneutical methods affirms this:

---

39 John Murray, *Divorce* (Philipsburg: Presbyterian and Reformed Publishing Co., 1961), 5-6.

40 Ibid., 6. He cites examples from C. F. Keil and F. Delitzsch, S. R. Driver, and Joseph Reider, who all affirm this construction.

The New Testament is to control the Old, not the Old the New. This is an important axiom, for revelation is progressive, and the final statement is in the New Testament. So the Old can, indeed, be poured through the New in an attempt to expound its meaning...the Old Testament is replete with doctrinal teaching. But the doctrine has to be refined and brought to its fullest expression as it is in the New. So it is important that this hermeneutic is clearly seen and employed by the preacher as he expounds the Scriptures. The New Testament will control the Old. He [Martyn Lloyd-Jones] believed that adherents of reformed theology particularly ran the risk of reversing this order.[41]

This is precisely what I see Instone-Brewer doing in *Divorce and Remarriage in the Bible*. It is a phenomenal work of research that I have learned much from, but his conclusions can be dismissed because he commits this hermeneutical mistake, among others. His research is great. His hermeneutics are not so great.

Essentially, he argues that an Old Testament passage (Exodus 21:10–11) that regulates the treatment of concubines sold into slavery implies certain conditions of the marriage covenant. These conditions are that the man must not neglect the woman's physical and emotional needs: "He shall not diminish her food, her clothing, and her marriage rights" (Exodus 21:11). If these conditions are broken, then a divorce may legitimately occur, and a remarriage is assumed to be lawful. This is Instone-Brewer's interpretation, which differs from some commentators'.[42]

He then takes his understanding of this passage and believes that it is implied in every passage in the New Testament where Jesus and Paul discuss divorce and remarriage. This understanding essentially makes divorce and remarriage lawful in virtually every case, with, of course, the exception of burning the toast! The only reason it's not OK to divorce and remarry is if

---

41 Tony Sargent, *The Sacred Anointing: The Preaching of Dr. Martyn Lloyd-Jones* (Wheaton: Crossway Books, 1994), 227.

42 *Keil and Deilitzsch Commentary on the Old Testament, Volume 2* (Peabody: Hendrickson Publishers, 1996), 131.

spouses don't put their socks in the laundry hamper, but even then I think we could gin up some emotional neglect! Thank you, Instone-Brewer.

Other considerations ought to be mentioned here regarding the supremacy of the New Covenant over the Old. The entire Epistle to the Hebrews is an apologetic for the supremacy of the New Covenant over the Old.

> But now He has obtained a more excellent ministry, inasmuch as He is also Mediator of a better covenant, which was established on better promises. For if that first covenant had been faultless, then no place would have been sought for a second. Because finding fault with them, He says: "Behold, the days are coming, says the Lord, when I will make a new covenant with the house of Israel and with the house of Judah." (Hebrews 8:6–8)

John Owen's remarks on this passage are helpful:

> The reasons for fixing the distinction in the first place are, (1) because μεμφόμενος, "finding fault," answers directly to οὐκ ἄμεμπτος, "was not without fault." And this contains the true reason why the new covenant was brought in. It was not God's complaint of the people that was any cause of the introduction of a new covenant, but of the old covenant itself, which was insufficient to sanctify and save the church.[43]

Prior to Jesus's total prohibition of divorce and remarriage in the Gospel of Luke, he affirms that he is not abolishing the law. Matthew Henry's comments on this passage (Luke 16:17–18) help elucidate how the New Covenant is better than the Old, not by abolishing it but by perfecting it.

> Yet still he protests against any design to invalidate the law (Luke 16:17): It is easier for heaven and earth to pass, *parelthein*—to pass

---

43 *The Works of John Owen, Volume 16* (Carlisle: Banner of Truth, 1991), 222.

by, to pass away, though the foundations of the earth and the pillars of heaven are so firmly established, than for one tittle of the law to fail. The moral law is confirmed and ratified, and not one tittle of that fails; the duties enjoined by it are duties still; the sins forbidden by it are sins still. Nay, the precepts of it are explained and enforced by the gospel, and made to appear more spiritual. The ceremonial law is perfected in the gospel colours; not one tittle of that fails, for it is found printed off in the gospel, where, though the force of it is as a law taken off, yet the figure of it as a type shines very brightly, witness the epistle to the Hebrews. There were some things which were connived at by the law, for the preventing of greater mischiefs, the permission of which the gospel has indeed taken away, but without any detriment or disparagement to the law, for it has thereby reduced them to the primitive intention of the law, as in the case of divorce (Luke 16:18), which we had before, Matt. 5:32; 19:9. Christ will not allow divorces, for his gospel is intended to strike at the bitter root of men's corrupt appetites and passions, to kill them, and pluck them up; and therefore they must not be so far indulged as that permission did indulge them, for the more they are indulged the more impetuous and headstrong they grow.[44]

Christ's law strikes at the heart of sin in man; it does not merely manage sin, as some aspects of the law had formerly done. John Calvin's commentary on Exodus 21:7–11, the same passage Instone-Brewer relies heavily on, makes similar points as well.

> From this passage, as well as other similar ones, it plainly appears how many vices were of necessity tolerated in this people. It was altogether an act of barbarism that fathers should sell their children for the relief of their poverty, still it could not be corrected as might have been hoped. Again, the sanctity of the marriage-vow should have been

---

44 Matthew Henry's Commentary on Luke 16:17–18 available at biblegateway.com.

greater than that it should be allowable for a master to repudiate his bond-maid, after he had betrothed her to himself as his wife; or, when he had betrothed her to his son, to make void that covenant, which is inviolable: for that principle ought ever to hold good—"Those whom God hath joined together, let not man put asunder" (Matthew 19:6; Mark 10:9). Yet liberty was accorded to the ancient people in all these particulars; only provision is here made that the poor girls should not suffer infamy and injury from their repudiation.[45]

Again, Calvin makes a similar observation in his commentary on Deuteronomy 24:1:

Although what relates to divorce was granted in indulgence to the Jews, yet Christ pronounces that it was never in accordance with the Law, because it is directly repugnant to the first institution of God, from whence a perpetual and inviolable rule is to be sought. It is proverbially said that the laws of nature are indissoluble.[46]

Calvin acknowledges certain indulgences in the Old Covenant that are done away with in the New. Furthermore, he notes that the New Covenant commands simply restored what was morally binding since the creation of the world, because the laws of nature cannot be altered. Lastly, I would like to provide an extensive quote from James Jordan that I believe to be tremendously helpful here, as it describes the "eschatological character" of the law.

What is "good" at an early stage of history may not still be "good" later. A drawing by a child may be evaluated "very good" by adults, but the same crudities from the hand of an adult would not be given

---

45 John Calvin, "Commentary on Exodus 11," *Calvin's Commentary on the Bible* (1840-57). https://www.studylight.org/commentaries/cal/exodus-21.html
46 John Calvin, "Commentary on Deuteronomy 24," *Calvin's Commentary on the Bible* (1840–57). //www.studylight.org/commentaries/cal/deuteronomy-24.html.

the same evaluation. It is important to affirm the eschatological character of the good, because it helps to explain the fact that the products of human work do not endure.

It also explains why each stage of the Old Covenant was good and wonderful at the time, but yet needed to be superseded later on. The New Testament speaks disparagingly of the Old Covenant, using such phrases as "weak and worthless elementary principles" (Galatians 4:9), "milk for babes" (Hebrews 5:13), and the like; but only in comparison with the New Covenant. In 1400 B.C., the Mosaic Covenant was the most wonderful thing in the world (Deuteronomy 4:6–8). But what is good for a child is not necessarily still good for an adult, and it is perverse to cling to childish things (Galatians 4:1–11; 1 Corinthians 13:11).[47]

Harmonizing these things is challenging, but the harmonization provided by Calvin, Owen, Henry, and especially Jordan is valuable in addressing the difficulties raised by the management of polygamy and divorce in the Old Testament. The law of the Lord is perfect, and it perfectly managed certain sinful behavior to prevent further sinful behavior, until the perfection of the New Covenant arrived. It was a schoolmaster for a petulant and infantile Church, but we have passed into maturity now. The New Covenant clarifies and expounds the law so that monogamous marriage, one man and one woman for life, just as it was in the beginning, is not just the ideal but the reality of marriage. We can try to justify ourselves and return to Moses, to put our trust in Moses, but if we believe Moses, then we must believe Jesus. And Jesus appeals to the created order in Genesis as the reality of the marriage covenant.

When you get into the deep things of God, it's like entering into quantum mechanics. Sometimes doctrines leave as particles and arrive as waves. In other words, God's law doesn't always fit into neat and tidy categories. It is, nevertheless, able to be apprehended and capable of being obeyed.

---

47 James Jordan, *Through New Eyes* (Eugene: Wipf and Stock Publishers, 1999), 123.

God Is Divorced and Remarried, So It's Cool

When adulterous-marriage apologists can't make their case with the explicit teachings of Jesus and Paul, they try to argue through the analogy of Christ and the Church. To use this analogy is acceptable in understanding marriage ethics, so I don't take issue with this approach when done properly. Paul uses it in his letter to the Ephesians to teach on marriage. Men are to love their wives as Christ loved the Church and gave Himself up for her, and women are to submit to their husbands as the Church submits to Christ, because the husband is the head of the woman as Christ is the head of the Church. There are aspects of Christ's marriage to the Church that we are to emulate in our human marriages.

However, the covenantal relationship is not identical in every way. For example, the covenant God made with His people is eternal. The covenants men and women make in marriage are not. Christians are not Mormons who believe that human marriages transcend death. God is able to exercise forms of punishment on His wife that men are not allowed to do. Women are allowed to disobey their husbands if their husbands tell them to sin, but the Church is never allowed to disobey her husband. In Jeremiah 3, God refers to the people He is married to as children, and He is in covenant with Judah, Israel's sister as well, yet we don't take this as prescription for us to marry children or for polygamy. So because there are similarities and dissimilarities, we need to understand that our starting point for prescriptive application begins with what Jesus taught regarding divorce and remarriage and that everything else supplements those teachings. Analogous relationships are a step removed from direct commands. This must be kept in mind.

The argument that God is divorced and remarried and it is therefore OK for us to divorce and remarry revolves around the transition from the Old Covenant to the New Covenant. The argument goes something like this: God was married to Israel in the Old Covenant. God divorces Israel in the New Testament because she is unfaithful, and He remarries the Church. God divorced and remarried for lawful reasons, just as Jesus says in Matthew 19:9!

The main problem with this argument is that it disregards the fact that death is required in order for there to be a New Covenant. There is not one single person who enters into the New Covenant without dying first. Jesus, the God-Man, dies and, in His resurrection, brings forth the New Covenant. And anyone who wants to be part of the New Covenant has to die through baptism and be resurrected into that covenant. This is precisely the point Paul is making in Romans 7:1–6:

> Or do you not know, brethren (for I speak to those who know the law), that the law has dominion over a man as long as he lives? For the woman who has a husband is bound by the law to her husband as long as he lives. But if the husband dies, she is released from the law of her husband. So then if, while her husband lives, she marries another man, she will be called an adulteress; but if her husband dies, she is free from that law, so that she is no adulteress, though she has married another man. Therefore, my brethren, you also have become dead to the law through the body of Christ, that you may be married to another—to Him who was raised from the dead, that we should bear fruit to God. For when we were in the flesh, the sinful passions which were aroused by the law were at work in our members to bear fruit to death. But now we have been delivered from the law, having died to what we were held by, so that we should serve in the newness of the Spirit and not in the oldness of the letter.

What is necessary for entry into the New Covenant? Death. One must die in Christ through baptism and be resurrected into new life as a new person who is part of the bride of Christ, the Church. "Or don't you know that all of us who were baptized into Christ Jesus were baptized into his death? We were therefore buried with him through baptism into death in order that, just as Christ was raised from the dead through the glory of the Father, we too may live a new life" (Romans 6:3–4). Paul even compares this to the law of marriage. A woman is bound by law to her husband as long as he lives. The only thing that releases her is his death.

So it is misleading to say that God divorces Israel and marries the Church. A case *might* be made that He divorces Israel and then she is justly killed for her perpetual unfaithfulness. But either way, death is required for a new covenant.

It has been argued that Jesus divorces Old Covenant Israel in the book of Revelation. The argument is that after Jesus issues the seven letters to the seven churches in Asia, He issues an eighth letter, which is a certificate of divorce to the unfaithful harlot, Jerusalem, representing Old Covenant Israel. While it may be plausible that this happens in Revelation, one must still deal with the fact that Jesus kills His old bride; He destroys the unfaithful harlot, Jerusalem. You might even argue that Jesus hires a hitman, Rome, to kill her (Revelation 17:16–17, 18–19). I don't want to argue this way. I only say it because if one wants to start arguing that Jesus divorces and remarries, you have to accept that Jesus also kills His old wife—and He kills her before He marries His new wife. So even if we accept this line of reasoning, which I am hesitant to do, it still supports the idea that marriage is ended only in death.

Another difficulty here is the mystery of the relationship between Israel and the Church. Those who subscribe to covenantal theology see more continuity between the Old and New Testaments and generally believe the Christian Church to be virtually synonymous with Israel. Israel and the Church are the same. I lean heavily in this direction, and it is always surprising to me when covenantal theologians argue that Jesus divorces Old Covenant Israel to marry the Church. On the other hand, dispensational theologians view Israel and the Church as much more distinct entities. I am sympathetic with this view too. Both are true in my opinion.

Paul argues that both are true in Romans 9–11. True Israel, the Israel of God (Galatians 6:16), is made up of those who have the faith of Abraham, whether they are Jews or gentiles (Galatians 3:7). The Church and Israel are the same. And yet he also affirms that Old Covenant Israel is still a distinct entity, because Old Covenant Israel was entrusted with the law and the prophets, and they are the enemies of New Covenant Israel for the gospel's sake but beloved because they are elect for the sake of the patriarchs (Romans 11:28). He calls this a mystery and past finding out (Romans 11:25, 11:33–35). And it is.

So when we start using these relationships to argue for or against divorce and remarriage, it becomes difficult. It should be something that reinforces what Jesus explicitly taught, not a starting point for modifying it.

I Wasn't a Christian, So It Isn't Adultery

Another objection that is often put forward is that God's law doesn't apply to non-Christians. One form of this objection is that a Christian who simply didn't know should be excused because of ignorance at the time. Others will say that we are new creatures in Christ, so it's as if the divorce and remarriage never happened. "I wasn't a Christian at the time, so my remarriage isn't adultery." That's the argument.

First, the marriage covenant is not a sacrament in the strict sense of the word, which means that the Church does not hold exclusive rights in administering it. It's a creational ordinance that God has always recognized among nonbelievers. The marriages of Cain, Lamech, Abimelech, Potiphar, Ahab, Daniel's accusers, Philip the Tetrarch, Pilate, those who lived during the days of Noah, and unbelievers married to Christians are all recognized by God as legitimate (Genesis 4:17, 4:19, 20:17, 39:9; 1 Kings 16:31, 21:5, 21:7, 21:25; Daniel 6:24; Matthew 14:3–4; Matthew 27:19; Luke 17:27; 1 Corinthians 7:10–16). The marriage standard applies to unbelievers and believers alike.

If I steal a car as a nonbeliever and then become a Christian, is it OK to keep the car? Does my conversion magically legitimize my theft? Do I simply need to be a good steward of the car that I stole? That's the exact logic Christians use to justify stolen wives and husbands.

Second, when someone enters into a covenant with God or with God as witness, it's objectively binding until death. Comparing the covenant entered into at baptism with the covenant entered into at marriage may prove helpful here.

When you are baptized into Christ, you are a Christian until you die. Nothing will change your objective status as a baptized Christian. When the terms of the covenant are broken, it doesn't dissolve the covenant or nullify the baptism; rather, it brings curses instead of blessings for violating the covenant (Hebrews 10:26–31; Deuteronomy 28) and, ultimately, damnation if there is no repentance (John 15:5–6). Paul appeals to a Christian's baptism into Christ as a reason not to sin. He doesn't argue that sin is a reason for the baptism to become void (Romans 6:1–4).

Similarly, when you are covenantally bound to your spouse, you are a spouse until you die. When you conduct a wedding ceremony, place the ring on your finger, exchange vows (which usually include "till death do us part"), and consummate the marriage, you are a husband or wife until you die. The marriage ceremony is like a baptismal ceremony. It's an external ritual indicating a spiritual reality. The covenant that was made in marriage, as in baptism, is a reason not to sin by violating the terms of the covenant. Violating the terms of the covenant is not a reason for the covenant to become void.

A husband may say, "I renounce marriage. I don't believe in my wife anymore. I'm going to sleep around now." But it doesn't mean that he is no longer a husband. He's just an unfaithful husband. He's an apostate husband.

Similarly, a Christian may say, "I renounce my marriage to Christ. I don't believe in God. I'm going to sin up a storm." But it doesn't mean that he or she is no longer a Christian. That person is just an unfaithful Christian, an apostate Christian.

Unfaithfulness doesn't change the fact that the person was objectively brought in and marked out as God's through baptism or objectively marked out as a husband or wife through marriage. Rather, the person's unfaithfulness makes the curses more severe because of the baptism or marriage.

The obligations upon a person due to citizenship are also similar. Those born in the United States are, by virtue of their births, Americans. They may say, "I'm no longer an American, and I'm going to fight with ISIS." But those words or actions do not make their citizenship go away. Rather, their citizenship makes those words or actions treason.

Marriage is a covenant that exists objectively and applies equally to all people. It is not dependent on whether someone confesses to or believes in Christ at the time. It doesn't matter whether someone is truly regenerate at the time. The covenant made in marriage is not contingent on these things. Therefore, the words of Christ are affirmed when He says, "*Whoever* divorces his wife and marries another commits adultery against her" (Mark 10:11, emphasis mine) and "*whoever* marries her who is divorced commits adultery" (Matthew 19:9, emphasis mine).

What about Love (and Grace)? Don't Let It Slip Away

This is the weakest objection, but you'd be surprised by the frequency and fervency with which I've heard it, which reveals the confusion evangelicals have about love and grace. It also reveals how the modern position on divorce and remarriage bastardized the words *love* and *grace*, which then greased the skids for the tolerance of sodomite marriages and transgenderism and, eventually, every form of sexual deviancy. In essence, conservative Christians, when it comes to divorce and remarriage, are proto-libtards.

Sodomite churches are open and affirming because conservative churches are too. Conservative churches are open and affirming of adulterous marriages. When people say that the traditional teaching on divorce and remarriage is not gracious or loving, they are making the *exact* same argument that liberal Christians make for homosexual marriages. Liberal Christians are able to make this argument because conservative Christians made it first.

The liberal Christian argues that it is not gracious or loving to exclude people from the Christian community and prevent them from being "happy" by being with the people they "love" simply because of the way God made them. How on earth will they survive without orgasms? Unacceptable. Yes, it may be a sin, they say, but God is gracious and can overcome sin. God is so gracious that no sin is too big for him to overcome, even blatant unrepentant rebellion apparently.

This is the *exact* way some defenders of adulterous marriages argue. They just repeat the preceding argument, but instead of defending homosexual marriages, they defend adulterous marriages. And the LGBTQXYZ666#*$% community clearly sees the hypocrisy of Christians here.

The remaining Christians who still publicly declare that it is unlawful for homosexuals to marry are demonized by liberals as being hateful and bigoted.

But these conservative Christians know they are not. They are simply affirming what the word of God says, which is a gracious and loving thing to do.

Similarly, when Christians who believe in traditional marriage publicly declare that it is unlawful for anyone to divorce and remarry, they are demonized by fellow conservative Christians as being ungracious, legalistic, hateful, and unloving. But they are not. They are simply affirming what the word of God says. They are being gracious and loving in the correct biblical sense.

When we use the words *grace* and *love* in a way that winks at sin, we are using these words in a bastardized sense. We are not being true to the word of God, because we are not employing the concepts in the same way Scripture does.

Grace means many things in Scripture, but it has generally been described as God's unmerited favor toward sinners. I think this is a fair definition. "For by grace you have been saved through faith, and that not of yourselves; it is the gift of God, not of works, lest anyone should boast. For we are His workmanship, created in Christ Jesus for good works, which God prepared beforehand that we should walk in them" (Ephesians 2:8–10).

Notice that grace saves us unto good works. We aren't given grace and saved so that we can continue in sin. The transliterated Greek word here for grace is *charis*. The Hebrew equivalent is *hen*. "Noah found grace in the eyes of the Lord" (Genesis 6:8). Noah didn't use God's grace toward him as an occasion to sin. Instead, he obeyed the word of God and built an ark out of faithful obedience, which then resulted in his salvation from the destructive floodwaters.

Some translations use the word *favor* instead of *grace*. It is found in a variety of contexts throughout Scripture, but it is never used as a reason to continue in sin. In the Epistle to the Hebrews, Paul warns the Jews who desire to return to the ritualistic sacrifices of the Old Covenant about what will happen if they continue in willful sin and insult the Spirit of grace.

For if we sin willfully after we have received the knowledge of the truth, there no longer remains a sacrifice for sins, but a certain fearful expectation of judgment, and fiery indignation which will devour the adversaries. Anyone who has rejected Moses' law dies without mercy on the testimony of two or three witnesses. Of how much worse punishment, do you suppose, will he be thought worthy who has trampled the Son of God underfoot, counted the blood of the covenant by which he was sanctified a common thing, and insulted the Spirit of grace? For we know Him who said, "Vengeance is Mine, I will repay," says the Lord. And again, "The Lord will judge His people." It is a fearful thing to fall into the hands of the living God. (Hebrews 10:26–31)

While the sin being addressed here is particular to the covenantal transition, the principle can be applied to any unrepentant sin or wrong worship. When people refuse to repent of their sins or willingly decide to worship in an unlawful way after being illumined by the truth, they are bringing severer judgment on themselves for violating the Spirit of grace than if they were merely violating the Law of Moses. Notice that the punishment for unrepentant sin is harsher in the New Covenant. Let me say that again: punishments are harsher in the New Covenant.

Paul makes a similar point in Romans after comparing the sin that reigned under the law and the grace that reigns under Christ: "What shall we say then? Shall we continue in sin that grace may abound? Certainly not! How shall we who died to sin live any longer in it?" (Romans 6:1–2). Grace is a reason to flee from sin, not a reason to continue in it.

Grace doesn't mean that God lightened up in the New Testament. It doesn't mean that God is more relaxed with your sin now that Jesus took care of it for you. Rather, those who continue to sin willfully after receiving the knowledge of the truth no longer receive the benefits of Christ's sacrifice. And those who do receive God's grace turn away from sin and are zealous for good works. Paul describes it this way:

For the grace of God that brings salvation has appeared to all men, teaching us that, denying ungodliness and worldly lusts, we should live soberly, righteously, and godly in the present age, looking for the blessed hope and glorious appearing of our great God and Savior Jesus Christ, who gave Himself for us, that He might redeem us from every lawless deed and purify for Himself His own special people, zealous for good works. (Titus 2:11–14)

This true meaning of grace is not what is meant when people say that the traditional interpretation of divorce and remarriage is not gracious. And if they do, then they fail to understand how the traditional teaching extends grace to the sinners in adulterous marriages.

Those in adulterous marriages may receive grace if they repent of their adultery by separating themselves from whomever they are committing adultery with. It is God's grace that someone would inform them of their sin. "Or do you presume on the riches of his kindness and forbearance and patience, not knowing that God's kindness is meant to lead you to repentance?" (Romans 2:4). This is what grace looks like.

Another objection or misunderstanding in this general area of confused liberal thinking by conservative Christians is that the traditional view of divorce and remarriage teaches that it is the unforgiveable sin. The fact that this is a frequent objection is astounding to me.

So let's clear up the confusion. All sin is unforgiveable if you don't repent of it. We must strive against sin and resist it at all times. Sin is crouching at our door and its desire is to have us, but we must master it (Genesis 4:7). If we fail, we confess ours sin and forsake it (1 John 1:9, Romans 6:1-4). But we never accept it and it affirm it. We cannot live lawless lives and expect forgiveness. Those who practice lawlessness will not inherit the kingdom (1 Corinthians 6:9). Even if we do mighty works for the kingdom and yet practice lawlessness, Jesus will say, "I never knew you; depart from Me, you workers of lawlessness" (Matthew 7:23). If I murdered someone every day of my life without ever confessing the sin, without ever asking God's forgiveness, and without ever repenting by discontinuing my murderous habit, it would be an unforgiveable sin. Divorce and remarriage is an ongoing sin. The marriage itself is adultery and therefore intrinsically sinful. It is committing the act of adultery every day. Repent of it by forsaking it, and be forgiven.

We've dealt with grace. Now, what about love? How do divorce-remarriage apologists bastardize the word *love*? They do so by claiming it is unloving to call adulterers to repentance from the unlawful marriages. This is too burdensome and unloving a requirement. How will they ever live single lives? How will they ever find happiness alone? What about the children?

But the Lord says obeying God is not a burden. Obeying God is loving. It is how you love God. "By this we know that we love the children of God, when we love God and keep His commandments. For this is the love of God, that we keep His commandments. And His commandments are not burdensome" (1 John 5:2–3).

Paul says that adulterers will not inherit the kingdom of God (1 Corinthians 6:9). Is it loving to God and to these adulterers to tell them that they can remain in their sin? Or does it demonstrate love to tell them that if they continue in their sin, they will not inherit the kingdom of God? It is more loving to warn them and to call them to repentance, because this offers eternal life to them in Christ.

If my friend's father were a millionaire and I alone discovered that in his father's last will and testament, it was declared that my friend, a senior at Ohio State University, would not receive his inheritance if he graduated from Ohio State University, I would strongly urge him to withdraw, and not just because I'm a Michigan fan.

Would it be loving to keep this information to myself? Perhaps you're of the mind that money is the root of all evil (which it is not) and it might be loving to keep the information to yourself, so let us change the metaphor.

Suppose there were a small child in a burning house who didn't want to leave because he really loved a mural he painted in his room. This mural was beautiful, and it reminded him of God's goodness. Would it be loving to let him stay in the burning house because the mural made him happy and he didn't want to part with it? Or would it be loving to yell at the kid to leave and drag him out of the house kicking and screaming if he didn't comply?

Our bastardized use of the word *love* would recommend we whisper, "I love you, sweet child. I'm glad you're happy," pat him on the head, and exit the crumbling inferno while congratulating ourselves for how much we show the love of Christ to people.

Those who are divorced and remarried will not inherit the kingdom of heaven. They forfeit their inheritance for a bowl of soup if they continue in their unlawful marriages. The lack of grace and love is committed by those who stand by and say nothing. The lack of grace and love is committed by those who speak comforting lies to these sinners as they approach hell. The lack of grace and love is found in the person who defends a doctrine that leads God's people into sin. "By her teaching she misleads my servants into sexual immorality" (Revelation 2:20).

Why Obsess over This? What about Other Sin?

What makes divorce and remarriage different from other sins is that it is the one sin in conservative churches that is affirmed and perpetuated as a good thing. Other sins like lying and stealing might be happening in the Church, but they are not defended or condoned by the leadership. We don't get together and have ceremonies celebrating masturbation, lust, theft, murder, or bearing false witness. But we do when it comes to the adultery of divorce and remarriage. "Woe to those who call evil good and good evil, who put darkness for light and light for darkness, who put bitter for sweet and sweet for bitter!" (Isaiah 5:20).

CHAPTER 3

YOUR PASTOR IS AN ORGY REFEREE

———

Our love is disordered. Until it is rightly ordered, we will not resolve this problem. Our love for our friends, family, church, and pastors is what makes this issue difficult and offensive. It is not an intellectual hurdle we are looking to jump; it is an emotional mountain we are unable to climb. How could so many people who love the Lord and who bear seemingly good fruit be in sin or in favor of sin? This, admittedly, has been the most difficult aspect for me as well. I'll offer a few biblical examples to, hopefully, help us work through this.

In the Gospel of Matthew, Peter is commended for speaking the magnificent truth that Jesus is the Christ, but then is reprimanded almost immediately for speaking the satanic lie that Jesus did not have to go to the cross.

> When Jesus came into the region of Caesarea Philippi, He asked His disciples, saying, "Who do men say that I, the Son of Man, am?" So they said, "Some say John the Baptist, some Elijah, and others Jeremiah or one of the prophets." He said to them, "But who do you say that I am?" Simon Peter answered and said, "You are the Christ, the Son of the living God." Jesus answered and said to him, "Blessed are you, Simon Bar-Jonah, for flesh and blood has not revealed this to you, but My Father who is in heaven. And I also say to you that you are Peter, and on this rock I will build My church, and the gates of Hades shall not prevail against it. And I will give you the keys of the kingdom of heaven, and whatever you bind on earth will be bound in heaven, and whatever you loose on earth will be loosed in heaven." Then He commanded His disciples that they should tell no one that

He was Jesus the Christ. From that time Jesus began to show to His disciples that He must go to Jerusalem, and suffer many things from the elders and chief priests and scribes, and be killed, and be raised the third day. Then Peter took Him aside and began to rebuke Him, saying, "Far be it from You, Lord; this shall not happen to You!" But He turned and said to Peter, "Get behind Me, Satan! You are an offense to Me, for you are not mindful of the things of God, but the things of men." (Matthew 16:13–23)

In one instance, Peter is speaking profound truth revealed from the Father in heaven, and in the next, he is advocating for things that are contrary to the will of the Father. Then immediately after, Jesus explains the necessity of His crucifixion to His followers. Peter then rebukes Jesus! Can you imagine? His desire is for Christ to deny His cross. This is satanic. And yet he just confessed Jesus as the Messiah. This is heavenly.

It is a bizarre thing for one man to speak glorious truth and then to speak the satanic will of men. But this is *precisely* what many pastors are doing. It is a picture of what the Church, in general, is doing—denying the cross-bearing the Father is giving them and their congregants on the issue of divorce and remarriage. They are taking their congregants aside and saying, "Far be it from you, precious child; this shall not happen to you!" Or in other words, "You don't need to pick up your cross and remain single and pray for reconciliation with your husband. Go ahead and get married to someone else. Go find your Boaz!" Or "You don't need to separate from this adulterous marriage. God is gracious, so you can stay in this sinful covenant. There is no need for you to go to the cross." This is satanic. These pastors, while filled in many areas with insight that was revealed to them from heaven, are not mindful of the things of God on the issue of adulterous marriages. They are mindful of the things of men.

I love Peter, but I'm going to pick on him again. In Paul's letter to the Galatians, Paul recounts his public rebuking of Peter:

Now when Peter had come to Antioch, I withstood him to his face, because he was to be blamed; for before certain men came from James, he would eat with the Gentiles; but when they came, he withdrew and separated himself, fearing those who were of the circumcision. And the rest of the Jews also played the hypocrite with him, so that even Barnabas was carried away with their hypocrisy. But when I saw that they were not straightforward about the truth of the gospel, I said to Peter before them all, "If you, being a Jew, live in the manner of Gentiles and not as the Jews, why do you compel Gentiles to live as Jews? We who are Jews by nature, and not sinners of the Gentiles, knowing that a man is not justified by the works of the law but by faith in Jesus Christ, even we have believed in Christ Jesus, that we might be justified by faith in Christ and not by the works of the law; for by the works of the law no flesh shall be justified." (Galatians 2:11–16)

Paul censures Peter for threatening the gospel by changing whom he ate lunch with. What does lunch have to do with the gospel? In short, the gentiles had been brought into the covenant by faith in Christ, just as the Jews were, and were not obligated to perform those ceremonial aspects of the law that were fulfilled with the coming of the Messiah.

Basically, the gentiles didn't need to become Jewish. They needed only to have the faith of Abraham, a faith that trusted and obeyed God, which, paradoxically, made them true Jews. Abraham, trusting and obeying Christ after hearing the gospel, was justified prior to the giving of the law. No one is justified by the works of the law, or ever has been. All are justified by faith, and always have been. But the point I want to make is that something seemingly small, not eating lunch with some folks, was a threat to the gospel.

This issue of divorce and remarriage, which is seemingly small to some, is also a threat to the gospel. People often tell me things that, in essence, boil down to, "How does divorce and remarriage threaten the gospel?"

The false teaching on divorce and remarriage denies the gospel itself and is protected by other doctrines that deny the gospel too. It is protected by a doctrine that gives little room to suffering. It is protected by a doctrine of cheap grace. It is protected by a doctrine of no repentance. It is protected by a doctrine of unforgiveness. It is protected by a doctrine that limits the miraculous power of God to work in impossible situations. It is protected by men and women who love their friends and family more than Christ. It is protected by those who love the kingdom more than the king. The doctrine that allows divorce and remarriage denies the gospel and threatens it in multiple ways.

And so even though Christ forgave Peter for his denial of Him and Peter had been baptized by the Holy Spirit and had been designated the leader of the apostles and commissioned as the Apostle to the Jews, Paul still got in his face and blamed him for being a hypocrite. Likewise, we must get in the face of our adored leaders who are being hypocrites on this issue and who are not being straightforward about the truth of the gospel, just as Peter wasn't.

KINGS OF JUDAH

Like Peter, some of the kings of Judah exhibited both exemplary and not-so-exemplary behavior. Some of these kings are described as good and yet were also disobedient of God's command to tear down the high places. These high places were where the people of other religions worshiped before Israel occupied the land and where Israelites worshiped contrary to God's commands. God instructed Israel to tear down these high places and worship Him in a particular way, either in the tabernacle or in the temple.

> When you have crossed the Jordan into the land of Canaan, then you shall drive out all the inhabitants of the land from before you, destroy all their engraved stones, destroy all their molded images, and demolish all their high places; you shall dispossess the inhabitants of the land and dwell in it, for I have given you the land to possess. (Numbers 33:51–53)
>
> You shall utterly destroy all the places where the nations which you shall dispossess served their gods, on the high mountains and on the hills and under every green tree. (Deuteronomy 12:2)

When the Israelites first broke this command, they still worshiped Jehovah God, but this is not what God commanded. He wanted Israel to worship in Jerusalem in the temple, in the place where He dwelt, in the place with a designated altar, with fire provided from heaven, and with a high priest as mediator.

When Sennacherib sent the Rabshakeh with his army to speak to Hezekiah at Jerusalem, he attempted to persuade the people against their king by saying Hezekiah took away their ability to worship God at the high places: "But if you say to me, 'We trust in the Lord our God,' is it not He whose high places and whose altars Hezekiah has taken away, and said to Judah and Jerusalem, 'You shall worship before this altar in Jerusalem'" (Isaiah 36:7).

God was involved in and approved of the sacrifices offered in the tabernacle and the temple. The glory of the Lord appeared, and fire from heaven came down and consumed the offerings in both places (Leviticus 9:23–24; 2 Chronicles 7:1). These two instances are typological expressions of what happened at Pentecost, where fire from heaven rested on Christ's disciples, whose lives were acceptable sacrifices. The Christian himself is the tabernacle, the temple, and the sacrifice.

When Christians divorce and remarry to the glory of God, they are making the same mistake that the Israelites made when they worshiped to the glory of God at the high places. It doesn't matter that you want to worship God with your adulterous marriage. God will not accept your sacrifices, however costly they may seem to you. No amount of good deeds or sacrificial and loving displays to your unlawful spouse will be received as acceptable worship by the Lord. Just as God was not involved in or approving of the worship at the high places, by not sending fire down from heaven, the fire of the Holy Spirit is not involved in or approving of your adulterous marriage. The tongues of flame do not rest on your rebellion.

This type of worship with adulterous marriage is contrary to the worship God has commanded, just as the worship at the high places was contrary to the worship God commanded Israel. And yet we are told that certain kings of Judah had loyal hearts to God and nevertheless did not remove the high places.

Asa did what was right in the eyes of the Lord, as did his father David. And he banished the perverted persons from the land, and removed all the idols that his fathers had made. Also he removed Maachah his grandmother from being queen mother, because she had made an obscene image of Asherah. And Asa cut down her obscene image and burned it by the Brook Kidron. But the high places were not removed. Nevertheless Asa's heart was loyal to the Lord all his days. (1 Kings 15:9–15)

King Asa did a litany of God-honoring things. He did what was right in the eyes of the Lord. He even removed the high places in Judah (2 Chronicles 14:5). He excommunicated sinners from the land. He confronted the sins of his family by removing their idols and by dethroning his grandmother because she was worshiping obscenely. Yet he did not tear down the high places in Israel, most likely from the Northern Kingdom territory he acquired (2 Chronicles 15:17; 1 Chronicles 16:1–6). He also made a treaty with the king of Syria, instead of relying on the Lord, which resulted in more wars as punishment for his foolishness. And he oppressed some of the people at the time (2 Chronicles 16:7–10).

This is what the good pastors in the Church are doing. The conservative Bible-believing pastors are doing many good things in the eyes of the Lord in many areas. They have even removed some high places, but they have not removed all of them. And they have compromised with our enemies, resulting in unnecessary wars and oppression of God's people. The point is that a commendable king like Asa still made some bonehead mistakes, which he probably thought were shrewd and wise, just as our conservative pastors do. Well, you can divorce and remarry in the case of adultery *as if* the offending spouse were dead. Clever, but sinful.

Asa's son, Jehoshaphat, does many good things as well. He is commended for doing right in the eyes of the Lord, yet by the end of his reign, he ultimately fails to tear down the high places (1 Kings 22:42; 2 Chronicles 20:33, even though it looks as though he initially tore them down; 2 Chronicles 17:6), and he allies himself with the kings of Israel, Ahab and Ahaziah. Both are wicked men.

He is rebuked for this: "Should you help the wicked and love those who hate the Lord? Therefore the wrath of the Lord is upon you. Nevertheless good things are found in you, in that you have removed the wooden images from the land, and have prepared your heart to seek God" (2 Chronicles 19:2–3).

Notice that he is both rebuked for bringing on himself the wrath of the Lord and commended for obeying and seeking God. Because of his alliance with wickedness, his kingdom endeavors were frustrated: "Because you have allied yourself with Ahaziah, the Lord has destroyed your works" (2 Chronicles 20:37).

Our Bible-believing conservative pastors are trying to build the kingdom while refusing to tear down all the high places and being allied with wicked men. This is why the Church is losing so dramatically in the United States. You can go to war with the culture all you want. You can preach against abortion and same-sex marriage until you're blue in the face, but because you have allied yourself with adulterers, God will destroy, and is already in the process of destroying, your works.

King Amaziah illustrates this point too. He did what was right in the eyes of the Lord, yet he didn't take down the high places, where the people still sacrificed and burned incense (2 Kings 14:3–4). In fact, we are told that he did what was right but not like his father, King David, did—not with a loyal heart (2 Kings 14:3; 2 Chronicles 25:2). Amaziah was able to slaughter the Edomites, but he began to impetuously worship other gods after this (2 Chronicles 25:14–15). And so when he fought against the wicked northern kingdom of Israel, he was annihilated. The king of Israel was so successful against Amaziah that he was able to invade Judah and Jerusalem and plunder the king's house and the temple of the Lord (2 Kings 14:8–14; 2 Chronicles 25:24).

This is like our conservative Christian pastors and churches, who want to do right in the sight of the Lord by attempting to retake the parts of the Church that openly condone and practice homosexuality, abortion, state worship, race worship, feminism, and so forth. But their hearts are not fully loyal to the Lord, because the high places of divorce and remarriage still stand. In fact, their hearts are lifted up, just as Amaziah's heart was lifted up because of his victory over the Edomites. Our hearts are lifted up because of our Christian victories over the past five hundred years, particularly the victories won at the

Reformation. But your victories in the past are not reason to believe you will be victorious in your battles now. You can continue to fight the liberal wing of the Church, but you will continue to lose. Tear down the high places, and you will have success.

King Azariah is almost identical to Amaziah, except that the text strongly implies that he was struck with leprosy for not taking down the high places (2 Kings 15:1–5). King Jotham is similar, and we are told that the Lord sends the kings of Israel and Syria after Jotham's kingdom of Judah (2 Kings 15:34–37). This was also a consequence of not removing the high places. Though we are not explicitly told this, it's obvious and even necessary to infer that this is the case. God's patience with Judah and its tolerance of the high places was wearing thin, and He was judging Judah accordingly.

However, when King Hezekiah and King Josiah arrive on the scene, we witness a refreshing change of events. They were the two kings who did tear down the high places (2 Kings 18:4; 2 Chronicles 34:3). They are commended with the highest praise (2 Kings 18:5, 23:25). These men were not perfect either, but they were different in that they were the only ones to tear down the high places.

As a result, Hezekiah had tremendous success. King Hezekiah was given complete victory over the Philistines all the way to Gaza, and he successfully rebelled against the king of Assyria and did not serve him (2 Kings 18:7–8). He was able to withstand the Assyrian onslaught, which took Israel away, but Judah remained. Hezekiah prospered because of his faithfulness (2 Chronicles 31:21).

Prior to Josiah's reign, Mannasah reigned and committed extreme wickedness, and because of this, God eventually destroyed Judah despite Josiah's faithful subsequent reign. However, because of Josiah's faithful reign, God withheld judgment as long as Josiah was alive (2 Chronicles 34:27–28).

Most pastors are not like King Mannasah, who was extremely wicked. They are more like King Jotham or King Azariah. They are good people who are losing a war because they haven't taken down the high places. I believe the Spirit of the Lord is calling His undershepherds to be more like King Hezekiah and King Josiah. Take down the high places. Preserve God's people from the Assyrian invasion. Add more years to your life, as God added more years to Hezekiah's.

I catalog these instances to demonstrate that there can be good rulers who neglect important commandments. And the neglect of these commandments has detrimental effects on the kingdom. Conservative Bible-believing pastors are like this.

TOLERATING JEZEBEL

Just as some of the kings in Judah were commended for the good things they did while not remaining faithful in some areas, the church in Thyatira was ruled by a minister who also did good things but failed in some areas.

In the book of Revelation, Jesus speaks to the angel of the church in Thyatira (Revelation 2:19–23). Throughout this passage, *you* and *your* are always in the singular, and *angel* simply means messenger. Jesus is speaking to the messenger of God who watched over the people in Thyatira. In the Old Covenant, nations and cities were influenced, guarded, and ruled by spiritual beings (see Genesis 3:24, Exodus 12:23, 2 Samuel 24:16, 2 Kings 19:35, and Daniel 10:13). But in the New Covenant, all authority in heaven and earth was given to Christ, and He sought fit to delegate this authority to His messengers, His angels, who are we Christians, elders, and pastors. In other words, I interpret this passage to mean that Jesus speaks to the minister or pastor of this church in Thyatira.

He commends him for what he does, for his love and faith, for his service and perseverance, and for doing more than what he did when he first started. His ministry was growing. He was loving. He was faithful. But he was not faithful with everything.

Jesus goes on to say that the pastor tolerates the woman Jezebel, who causes the saints in Thyatira to commit sexual immorality by her teachings. She seduces them into this. This is a sobering rebuke. How can these things exist side by side?

This church was growing and had so many strengths. In other words, if we saw it today, we would say that God was blessing it. We would see that the pastor had serious love for God and that he had a growing mercy ministry, a thriving classical Christian school, and a beautiful liturgy for Sunday worship. Because of these things, we would say to ourselves, "How could God have anything against this?" It is inconceivable to think that this pastor could possibly tolerate anything like a Jezebel. But this is exactly what many pastors are doing.

The pastors of our churches tolerate the woman Jezebel by declining to confront adulterous marriage in any meaningful sense. This, in turn, causes the saints to commit sexual immorality, as in Thyatira. The spirit of Jezebel has a hold of the pastor who facilitates saints to enter into covenants of adultery. This is high-handed wickedness and rebellion against God.

The prophet Samuel says that rebellion is as the sin of witchcraft (1 Samuel 15:23), and the major sins that Jezebel perpetuated while ruling in Israel were whoredom and witchcraft (2 Kings 9:22). These are precisely the sins that the Church is committing and defending.

To praise the consummation of a person's spouse to someone else is to praise a crime worthy of death. And then to defend it and say it is good is rebellion. Isaiah says, "Woe to those who call evil good, and good evil; Who put darkness for light, and light for darkness; Who put bitter for sweet, and sweet for bitter!" (Isaiah 5:20).

To think that the sinners in the world were the first to start calling evil good and good evil is naïve. You are blind to reality and deaf to the voice of God if you don't comprehend that it was the sinners in the Church who first began to call evil good and good evil. When you attend the marriage ceremony of a divorced person, you are attending a gay-pride parade in nascent form. Your church may do many wonderful things, but if it tolerates this witchcraft and whoredom, you will be punished, just as the church in Thyatira was.

> And I gave her time to repent of her sexual immorality, and she did not repent. Indeed I will cast her into a sickbed, and those who commit adultery with her into great tribulation, unless they repent of their deeds. I will kill her children with death, and all the churches shall know that I am He who searches the minds and hearts. And I will give to each one of you according to your works. (Revelation 2:21–23)

The things written of the church in Thyatira were written as an example for our sake. Jesus warned them that if they did not repent, He would bring sickness and suffering to them, and He would kill their children. This is a sobering rebuke to a church that had so much good going on, just like our conservative churches today. Except we are not being warned that if we do not repent of our toleration of Jezebel, we will be judged, and I believe the judgment has already started. Our sin is causing actual physical effects to manifest in sickness and death, particularly in our children.

The Church is our mother (Galatians 4:26) and is supposed to be a place where children are born and nurtured, not made sick and murdered. The Church is now functioning as an antimother. She is supposed to beget children, not murder them. Every conservative Christian is concerned about ending abortion in this country, but it will not end until we first end the abortion happening in our local churches. By this, I mean putting to death that witch Jezebel who teaches and seduces the saints into sexual immorality. The Church tolerates that witch Jezebel, but God's word says, "Thou shalt not suffer a witch to live" (Exodus 22:18). Our toleration of this witch has turned every local church into a Planned Parenthood facility, where our children are subject to death, both spiritually and physically.

A similar kind of judgment occurs at the church in Corinth. Paul reminds the Corinthians that those who eat and drink of the Lord's Supper in an unworthy manner are guilty of the body and blood of the Lord and that they eat and drink judgment on themselves. When people do this, it causes weakness, sickness, and even death (1 Corinthians 11). This is not the way it should be.

God promises that when we serve Him, He will take sickness away from us, He will take miscarriages away from us, and He will take barrenness away from us (Exodus 23:26). I have seen a tragic amount of sickness, miscarriages, and barrenness in the Church, and I am convinced that most of these instances are connected to our sin of adulterous marriages.

I am not saying that every case is from disobedience. We have Job and the Tower of Siloam that show us otherwise. The nexus of God's judgments and blessings is never as predictable as we would like it to be. So I won't say that every case of sickness and death is a result of adulterous marriages.

But these passages and principles that bring punishment and death to those who are in rebellion do exist in God's word for a reason, and I do believe that many of the tragic things we see in our church communities are God's punishment for our disobedience. We have become accustomed to living under a curse, to having our children die, to being sick all the time, and to having cancer and disease, but the kingdom of God has many blessings for those who obey Jesus fully. We must affirm this, and I believe that we cannot even begin to imagine the blessings that will occur when we begin to walk in the fullness of God's law.

I have written these things to create a space in your mind that can apprehend the glory and the horror of what some pastors are responsible for. I am not optimistic that the current leadership in the Church will receive this rebuke. They have too much to lose. But the Lord can do what He wishes and grant repentance to anyone. So it is my prayer that the leadership will hear what the Spirit of the Lord is saying and be wise.

A wise person receives rebuke when he or she is wrong. It's hard for older men to accept rebuke. They are set in their ways. They have contributed to the kingdom and built kingdoms for themselves, and to admit fault is to discount some of their work. It tarnishes their legacy. But we should be much more concerned with God's kingdom than with our own. The Lord is calling Christians who are leaders to repent of their folly in this area. It is causing a lot of devastation, and you need only to confess you're wrong, repent, and seek forgiveness, and it will be given. Peter received the rebuke from Jesus and from Paul. He accepted it because he was wrong, and as my sister says, "If Peter can be corrected, then so can your pastor."

These words are not easy to accept, and they are not easy to write. We would like the world to be simply good guys and bad guys. Black hats and white hats. But as it turns out, it's much more complicated than that. It's much more terrifying than that. Hopefully, these biblical examples have provided helpful categories to anyone struggling with how to reconcile the truth of Scripture that is God's will and your Christian friends, family, church members, and pastors who are not speaking God's will when it comes to marriage and who are defending adulterous marriages.

CHAPTER 4

GOD HATES YOUR WORSHIP

———

So far we've established that your church is a whorehouse but one of those classy ones, that your objections to this reality are pitiful, and that your pastor has the heart of a soup kitchen volunteer but also doubles as the manager of a club called Sexual Chaos, which gathers together every Sunday morning. In light of this, we can confidently say that God hates your worship.

Homo Adorans

Faithful worship is more than simply whether you use electric guitars or choirs, grape juice or wine, psalters or projection screens on Sunday morning. Worship is our obedience to God in all things (Romans 12). This means that how we live our lives from Monday to Saturday outside of our local assemblies of worship on Sunday matters a great deal to the Lord. What we say, what we think, and what we do are our spiritual acts of worship, our daily sacrifices. Our worship is who we are.

The central acts of worship after the giving of the law at Sinai and prior to Christ were in the tabernacle and the temple. These acts of worship typified Christ and His sacrifice, and they also typified followers of Christ and the sacrifice they offer with their bodies: "Or do you not know that your body is the temple of the Holy Spirit who is in you, whom you have from God, and you are not your own? For you were bought at a price; therefore glorify God in your body and in your spirit, which are God's" (1 Corinthians 6:19–20). Paul is rebuking the Corinthians for committing sexual immorality by appealing to their bodies as the dwelling place of the Holy Spirit. The story arc of history is one that starts with God dwelling with man, God separating from man, and then God incrementally reestablishing that dwelling with man.

In the Garden of Eden, man had direct access to God. God walked with Adam. Our sin separated us from God. Adam (or mankind) was exiled from the garden and therefore lost intimacy with God.

Then, as history progressed, God began to gather for Himself a people. He saved Noah and his family. He called Abraham, Isaac, and Jacob. He saved Israel from Egypt. And then He commanded Moses to build a tabernacle for Him to dwell in. Once a year, the high priest of Israel was allowed to enter the Holy of Holies, or the Most Holy Place, where the presence of the Lord was (Hebrews 9:7). Then Solomon built a temple that surpassed the tabernacle in glory, but the people of Israel, with the exception of the high priest, were still unable to access the presence of the Lord.

Then the Messiah, Jesus, came and dwelt among men and offered Himself as a sacrifice for His people, thus reconciling God to His people, as indicated by the tearing of the temple veil that separated God's presence from His people. At Pentecost, God's Holy Spirit was poured out onto the men of Jerusalem. Now God dwells in all who confess and believe in Christ and have been baptized. This is why Paul says our bodies are temples of the Holy Spirit, because that is where God dwells. The house of the Lord is His people. His people are the house of the Lord. The story arc of redemptive history moves from intimate fellowship with God, to separation, to priestly mediators, and finally back to intimate fellowship, and then to final consummation in resurrection glory.

God has shown us these things to bring to bear the glory of God dwelling among us and within the individual members of His Church but also to bring to bear the repulsiveness of what it means to sin. When you sin sexually, you defile the temple of the Lord. You worship wrongly. God gave specific instructions for how to worship in the temple. He gave specific instructions for how to worship in your body, which the temple typified. Part of those instructions was not to divorce and remarry or to marry a divorced woman, which we do and approve of all the time. This is improper worship in the temple of the Lord. God is not pleased with this type of worship.

This is not to say that corporate worship on Sunday is unimportant. It is. God cares that both individual and corporate worship are acceptable. The Christians in Acts meet on the first day of the week to break bread (Acts 20:7). Paul gives instructions for how to partake in the Lord's Supper when Christians come together (1 Corinthians 11:17–34). He gives instructions for how to exercise spiritual gifts when gathered together (1 Corinthians 12–14). Jesus teaches at the temple (Luke 20:1, Luke 21:37, and John 7:28–29). In Hebrews, we are reminded not to neglect assembling together (Hebrews 10:25). So corporate acts of worship are important too.

The Church, collectively, is the bride of Christ. This concept is helpful in providing another way in which to view the importance of corporate worship. When a man and woman are married, they are in covenant with each other. The things they do on a day-to-day basis are important and reflect the way in which they fail or succeed in being faithful to their covenantal vows. But there are special occasions when the man will take his wife out for dinner at a nice restaurant, walk with her along the river, bring her flowers, or whatever it is that makes her feel loved and secure. And the wife will display her affection through respect and submission by honoring his decision making and being an indispensable helpmate to his mission of subduing the earth. And these things can culminate in physical unification. When these ritual preliminaries occur and they unite, there is a type of renewal of the covenant, a revivification of it, a liturgical reminder that they are one and that they belong to each other. "I am my beloved's and my beloved is mine" (Song of Songs 6:3).

In a similar way, when the bride of Christ gathers to offer sacrifices of thanksgiving and praise and to eat bread and drink wine in remembrance of what her husband, Christ, did for her, it serves to revivify her covenant with her Lord. We, as the bride of Christ, are reminded that we are united with Christ. I am my beloved's, and my beloved is mine.

But right now, the bride of Christ is a manipulative witch and a slut, and God hates when she comes to Him for covenant renewal. When you worship on Sunday, God hates it. This is what the Lord is saying to you and your pastor:

> Hear the word of the Lord, you rulers of Sodom; Give ear to the law of our God, you people of Gomorrah: "To what purpose is the multitude of your sacrifices to Me?" Says the Lord, "I have had enough of burnt offerings of rams and the fat of fed cattle. I do not delight in the blood of bulls, or of lambs or goats. When you come to appear before Me, who has required this from your hand, to trample My courts? Bring no more futile sacrifices; Incense is an abomination to Me. The new moons, the sabbaths, and the calling of assemblies—I cannot endure iniquity and the sacred meeting. Your new moons and your appointed feasts My soul hates; they are a trouble to Me, I am weary of bearing them. When you spread out your hands, I will hide My eyes from you; Even though you make many prayers, I will not hear. Your hands are full of blood. Wash yourselves, make yourselves clean; Put away the evil of your doings from before My eyes. Cease to do evil, learn to do good; seek justice, rebuke the oppressor; defend the fatherless, plead for the widow." (Isaiah 1:10–17)
>
> What use to me is frankincense that comes from Sheba, or sweet cane from a distant land? Your burnt offerings are not acceptable, nor your sacrifices pleasing to me. (Jeremiah 6:20)
>
> I hate, I despise your feast days, and I do not savor your sacred assemblies. Though you offer Me burnt offerings and your grain offerings, I will not accept them, nor will I regard your fattened peace offerings. Take away from Me the noise of your songs, for I will not hear the melody of your stringed instruments. (Amos 5:21–23)

This is exactly how God views your worship. Let that sink in. Remember this when you're confessing the Apostles' Creed, kneeling for confession, singing about how much God loves you, or petitioning God to heal our land. Remember that He thinks the worship of those who perpetuate and defend adulterous marriages is disgusting. He can't stand it.

Rid yourself of the filth of your sexual immorality and your facilitation of sexual immorality in the house of worship, and then worship the Lord. You pride yourself in the beauty of your sophisticated liturgy and sacramental theology, and then you approvingly go to weddings that Jesus would have dispersed with a whip of cords. You send your daughters to hell by giving them to men who are covenantally bound to other women, and you think it's justified because you have a piece of paper that says "Divorced." You are truly like the Pharisees of Jesus's day. You laugh and delight in your little kingdoms while your friends and family are committed adulterers. You are either deceived or cowards and hypocrites. God is not impressed with your vestments and the fact that you use wine in your communion cups instead of grape juice. He's still going to plague you with disease and miscarriage unless you repent. He already has. Wake up! Perhaps you prefer to live in your squalor, but the kingdom is greater than what you're willing to settle for.

We commit the same mistakes as the Pharisees.

> Woe to you, scribes and Pharisees, hypocrites! For you pay tithe of mint and anise and cumin, and have neglected the weightier matters of the law: justice and mercy and faith. These you ought to have done, without leaving the others undone. Blind guides, who strain out a gnat and swallow a camel! (Matthew 23:23–24)

We specialize in the minutiae. If only we would start to sing the Psalms during worship. If only we would better understand the significance of the sacraments. If only we would stop neglecting our children from coming to waters of baptism. We have theological wars over what ecumenical unity looks like, the conditionality versus the unconditionality of the covenant, the use of the term *common grace*, and on and on it goes.

These are things that are particular to certain Reformed circles. But every tribe has its mint and anise and cumin. It doesn't matter whether you're a low-church Anabaptist, a Pentecostal, a nondenominational evangelical, a Neo-Calvinist, a Baptist, a Lutheran, an Anglo-Catholic, or whatever. Maybe the issue is head coverings or skirt length. Maybe it's more missions. Maybe it's more ecstatic worship and more tongues speaking and miracles. Maybe it's more incense and candles and higher appreciation for tradition and history and liturgy. But God scoffs at the people who foolishly emphasize these things while ignoring the orgy that's occurring in the sanctuary.

We are professional camel swallowers. We are medics on a battlefield who have no idea how to triage casualties. We don't even know how to adequately treat the casualties that we do prioritize. Let me write a blog about the evils of homosexuality, which is like saying here's a Band-Aid for your blood-launching femoral artery wound. Let me switch to a church with a beautiful and historically rooted liturgy. Band-Aid. Let me preach a sermon on appreciating the goodness of creation. Band-Aid. Let's start by putting a tourniquet on that first, which is another way of saying let's start by repenting of our approval and practice of unlawful adulterous marriages first, and then we can go on to talk about these other pressing social issues or tertiary doctrinal issues like paedocommunion or the aseity of God or supra- versus infralapsarianism or the necessity of motion in divisible beings (or whatever irrelevant topic you Reformed Thomists like to nerd out about). Whatever you want. Just stop the bleeding first.

COULD I GET THAT INIQUITY COMBO SUPERSIZED?

The worship that God hates is not limited to the adulterous marriages we practice and approve of. One of my teachers once told me that sins are like grapes; they come in clusters. This is true of sinful doctrine too. It comes with other sinful doctrine. Our modern sinful doctrine of divorce and remarriage, which is a doctrine of demons, has collected most other demonic doctrines in the Church to insulate itself from meaningful attack and to perpetuate other sin. These doctrines are perversions of the gospel, and they have coalesced and manifested into the doctrine that allows divorce and remarriage. These sinful doctrines that accompany divorce and remarriage and pervert our worship are as follows:

Unforgiveness. When people divorce and do not desire to stay single and pray for reconciliation, as the law commands, they are making declarations of unforgiveness toward their spouses. There are, of course, circumstances where separation may be the only lawful option, as when the unbelieving spouse leaves or there is continuous, unrepentant adultery. But in these cases, the posture of Christians should be to desire reconciliation and restoration, and they will do this by remaining single until the estranged spouse is dead or reconciled. But when they divorce and desire to marry someone else, they have denied the doctrine of forgiveness. Without their forgiveness of others, Christ will not forgive them.

Unbelief. Defenders of adulterous marriages deny that God has the ability to change the hearts of people. When they say, "I tried every possible thing I could do to reconcile, but it just wasn't going to happen," they are denying the power of God, and they are lying. Did you try waiting? No. You didn't. You set up an arbitrary timeline and said, "I'm done waiting. I don't like being lonely. This means I can break my covenantal vows of forsaking all others and remaining faithful until death." And your pastor was there to help you in that.

God made the world out of nothing. He made a human out of dirt. He turned water to wine. He came back to life after being dead for three days. Surely, He has the ability to change the heart of your spouse and to give you the patience to wait. "For how do you know, wife, whether you will save your husband? Or how do you know, husband, whether you will save your wife?" (1 Corinthians 7:16). If the Lord in His providence does not change the heart of your spouse, then you were made a eunuch for the sake of the kingdom, and Jesus says that's OK. That is now your cross to bear. This is what pastors ought to be speaking to their congregants. Instead, they are in the business of assuring their congregants that it's OK to deny the crosses that Jesus is giving them. "And whoever does not take his cross and follow Me is not worthy of me" (Matthew 10:38).

Cheap grace. When people divorce and remarry, they must begin to preach the doctrine of cheap grace. This means that they believe grace is God winking at sin. It's a doctrine that teaches that God is OK with someone continuing in sin against His law because to keep His law is legalism. Bonhoeffer describes it this way: "Cheap grace is the grace we bestow on ourselves. Cheap grace is the preaching of forgiveness without requiring repentance, baptism without church discipline, Communion without confession…cheap grace is grace without discipleship, grace without the cross, grace without Jesus Christ, living and incarnate."[48] Cheap grace denies the necessity of keeping God's law and denies that anyone practicing lawlessness will be cast out of the kingdom of God.

Jesus says, "Not everyone who says to Me, 'Lord, Lord,' shall enter the kingdom of heaven, but he who does the will of My Father in heaven. Many will say to Me in that day, 'Lord, Lord, have we not prophesied in Your name, cast out demons in Your name, and done many wonders in Your name?' And then I will declare to them, 'I never knew you; depart from Me, you who practice lawlessness!'" (Matthew 7:22–23). This cheap grace is a de facto selective antinomianism.

The individual sin vacuum. Individual sin does not happen in a vacuum. Achan's sin reveals that sin has communal effects. When the sin of divorce and remarriage is not dealt with appropriately, it causes others to sin, and it opens up the Church to the leaven of sin. Paul warns that a little bit of sin can permeate through the whole community (1 Corinthians 5:6). To allow someone to remain in an unlawful marriage is to teach that divorce and remarriage is ultimately lawful. It may be frowned upon, but ultimately, one may divorce and remarry and still be in good standing in the Church. The pedagogical effect works like leaven.

These sins have all coalesced into what is now the great heresy of the Church.

THE FEEL-GOOD, SUBORDINATE CHRIST FOR COWARDS: A PORTRAIT OF OUR WORSHIP

The story of the Levite and his concubine in Judges 19 is a gruesome picture of our worship. A Levite took for himself a concubine from Bethlehem in Judah. The concubine left him and stayed at her father's house. The Levite went to

---

48 Dietrich Bonhoeffer, *The Cost of Discipleship* (New York: MacMillan Publishing Co., 1979), 47.

retrieve her. The father was reluctant to see his daughter and her husband, the Levite, leave, so he convinced the Levite to stay for several days. The Levite eventually left with his concubine. He decided against staying in Jerusalem, which at the time was occupied by Jebusites. Since they were not Israelites, he decided to stay near Gibeah, where Israelites from the tribe of Benjamin lived.

However, nobody from the town would provide hospitality and lodging for them, so they were going to stay in the open square of the city, but an old man from the mountains of Ephraim, who was staying in the city, offered his place for them to stay. As they were visiting with one another, Benjamites from the city surrounded the house, beat on the door, and demanded that the man give up the Levite so that they could sodomize him (similar to Genesis 19).

The man offered his virgin daughter and the Levite's concubine instead. The Benjamites didn't find this agreeable, but the man threw out the Levite's concubine, and the Benjamites gang raped her all night. They eventually left, and the concubine collapsed at the door of the house where the Levite was and placed her hands on the threshold. The Levite opened the door and said, "Get up and let us be going" (Judges 19:28), but there was no reply because she was dead. The Levite took her body to his house, cut it up into twelve pieces, and sent the pieces all throughout Israel. This precipitated a bloody civil war between Israel and the Benjamites.

Like any typological prophecy in Scripture, there is a primary fulfillment and then subsequent fulfillments or applications. Think of time as a pond, and prophecies as smooth stones thrown over the surface. The stone touches down at an initial point but then continues to skip along the surface, touching down at multiple points. Prophecies touch down and apply in various ways at various times.

This story is similar. I believe the primary fulfillment applies to the Jews' rejection of the Messiah, but it can also apply to the Church presently, which is also rejecting the Messiah. The concubine figures as Christ, which seems strange, but stay with me here. The Levite represents the Jewish leadership, and the man from Ephraim who hosts the Levite and the Benjamites represents the people of Israel, the laity.

The concubine is reluctant to go with her husband, and we are told that she "played the harlot against him and went away from him to her father's house at Bethlehem in Judah, and was there four whole months" (Judges 19:2). Matthew Henry notes, "The Chaldee reads it only that she 'carried herself insolently to him,' or 'despised him,' and, he being displeased at it, she went away from him." The Septuagint reads that "she was angry with him." The Vulgate omits the phrase altogether and just says "she left him."[49] The context indicates that there wasn't harlotry in the sense of sexual infidelity but only that she deserted him. It specifies that she returns to her father's house, where it would be unlikely for her to commit sexual immorality, and we are told that the Levite "arose and went after, to speak kindly to her and bring her back" (Judges 19:3). Were she committing harlotry in the sense of sexual infidelity, it is unlikely that the Levite would have this type of response. This makes the typological association with Christ less bizarre.

I believe the concubine's father represents God the Father. The father is reluctant to let his daughter go with the Levite. He convinces the Levite to stay with him for several days, eating food, drinking wine, and resting. This, I believe, is because the father knows what is going to happen to his daughter, just as God the Father knew what was going to happen to His Son. The heart of the Father is revealed here. It shows His love for His Son. It provides an insight into the love that permeates the Trinity.

When the concubine initially leaves her husband, we are told that she goes away to her father's house for four whole months. I believe the four months symbolize the four hundred years of silence between the Old Testament and the New Testament. At the end of the four hundred years, the Son leaves His Father's house to speak to His people. At the end of the four months, the concubine speaks to her husband again and leaves her father's house. The Levite also speaks kindly to her, which symbolizes God's people desiring a Messiah.

In both cases, the people of God unjustly murder the spouse. Jesus, the husband of the Church, is crucified by the ecclesiastical leadership and a mob. The concubine, the wife of the Levite, is raped and beaten to death because

---

49 Matthew Henry's Commentary on Judges 19 available at biblegateway.com.

the ecclesiastical leadership and his host offer her to a mob. The parallels of this story to Lot in Sodom and Gomorrah are also worth exploring, but we do not have time to get into that here.

This rejection of Christ by His Church is anticipated in Judges 19. It is a brutal depiction of rejecting Christ, which happened in the first century and is also happening now. The leadership of the Church is protected by men from Ephraim who are willing to give up their virgin daughters to satiate the will of God's rebellious people, who are nothing less than a rapacious mob, a ravenous wolf, which is what the name Benjamin means (Genesis 49:27). Instead, the leadership offers Jesus for the people to abuse and satisfy their uncontrolled sexual urges.

The relationship of the Levite to his concubine reflects the type of relationship that God's leadership now has with the gospel. The leaders of the Church treat Christ like a second-rate spouse, a concubine who is there only to make them feel good, to have sex with, and to offer up as a protective shield from their congregations.

The relationship between the concubine and the Ephraimite host is like that of those laypersons in the Church who also wrongfully use Christ as a shield to protect themselves from being overcome by their fellow Israelites. Just as the Ephraimite wrongfully used the Levite's concubine to defend the Levite from the mob, the average layperson will wrongfully use Christ to protect his or her pastor.

The relationship between the concubine and the Benjamite mob reflects the relationship between the gospel and the laity of the Church who are in sexual immorality. They use Christ only to satisfy their carnal desires. "Christ said I could marry this other man's wife." No, He did not. "Christ said I could divorce my husband and marry a better one." No, He did not. "My parents are divorced and remarried, and I really like them a lot, so they must not be adulterers, as Christ says they are. They must not need to repent, as Christ says they must. The gospel of grace allows my friends at church to marry divorced men and women because grace can do anything!"

The Church is filled with people who are essentially raping the gospel of Christ for their own benefit. Scripture talks about what happens to those who insult the Spirit of grace (Hebrews 10:29). You are not above being sent to hell for your infidelities or punished for your facilitations of such infidelities.

However, it is worth noting that we are not told whether the Levite and the man from Ephraim with whom he lodged were punished in any way. We are told only that the Benjamites who actually committed the sexual immorality were punished by the rest of Israel in several bloody battles, which we will address later. The fact that we are not told whether the Levite or his host was punished does not allow us to conclude that those who facilitate the rape and murder of the gospel of Christ will not be held accountable as well, as other Scriptures clearly teach that those who facilitate such things will be held accountable (Matthew 18:6, Mark 9:42, and Luke 17:2).

THE SIN OF PILATE

Christians all over the world regularly confess their beliefs by reciting the Apostles' Creed. Christians confess that Jesus suffered under Pontius Pilate. Pilate did the same thing as the man from Ephraim who hosted the Levite. He gave the mob something they wanted to satiate their demands. Pilate even attempted to distance himself from any guilt: "So when Pilate saw that he was gaining nothing, but rather that a riot was beginning, he took water and washed his hands before the crowd, saying, 'I am innocent of this man's blood; see to it yourselves'" (Matthew 27:24). Yet history has judged that Pilate was guilty of Jesus's blood.

And so it is with everyone who reads the words of Christ regarding the indissolubility of marriage and does nothing to prevent the suffering of the Word, of the gospel, of Christ's body. Multiple pastors have told me that they do not officiate marriage ceremonies when divorced persons are involved. Great! But their hands are not innocent of the blood that they are letting be shed of the people in their congregations who are already divorced and remarried. Their hands are not innocent of the blood that is being shed by their peers, other pastors, who are perpetuating the spiritual, and sometimes physical, genocide of their flocks. And for those who are not pastors, we are a nation of priests, and if your pastor is involved in this insanity and your friends and family and fellow churchmates approve of or are practicing adulterers, you are also not innocent of the blood that is being shed if you stand by and do nothing.

> When I bring the sword upon a land, and the people of the land take a man from their territory and make him their watchman, when he sees the sword coming upon the land, if he blows the trumpet and warns the people, then whoever hears the sound of the trumpet and does not take warning, if the sword comes and takes him away, his blood shall be on his own head. He heard the sound of the trumpet, but did not take warning; his blood shall be upon himself. But he who takes warning will save his life. But if the watchman sees the sword coming and does not blow the trumpet, and the people are not warned, and the sword comes and takes any person from among them, he is taken away in his iniquity; but his blood I will require at the watchman's hand. (Ezekiel 33:2–6)

In some baptismal rites, after the parents of the infant pledge to undertake the responsibilities of raising their Christian child in the nurture and admonition of the Lord, the congregation is asked whether they will assist the parents in this covenantal responsibility as well, and the congregation affirms by saying "Amen." How can anyone in that congregation abdicate the responsibility of being a lookout if the pastors and the parents fail to see the danger of giving their child away to marry someone who is divorced? Or to allow any number of deadly covenant-breaking adulterous unions to occur?

If you say, "I have washed my hands of this," you are only fooling yourself, and you are guilty of the blood of those deaths. God will require your blood if you do not sound the trumpet of truth and warn of the danger. This holds for every single relationship you have. The elders at your church will be held responsible to a greater degree, but you will not be held unaccountable. Your silence is like the silence of those who knew what was happening at Auschwitz and Buchenwald and did nothing. Your silence only facilitates the murder of your brothers and sisters. And when God asks you where your brothers and sisters are, you cannot reply with, "Am I my brother's keeper?" (Genesis 4:9) or "That's what my pastor is for. I'm not a pastor. It's not my job to protect my Christian brothers and sisters from danger." It's not going to fly, and there will be blood on your hands. We have the word of God given to us and available to us, and passing off the responsibility to your pastor or institutional structures is just a way to abdicate responsibility. It's a way to hide.

God hates our worship because it consists of worshiping God in adultery and cowardice. "The sacrifice of the wicked is abomination to the Lord, but the prayer of the upright is His delight" (Proverbs 15:8). God is looking for people to worship him in spirit and in truth (John 4:24). But when you walk in darkness, you lie and do not practice truth (1 John 1:6). We are lying when we say that an adulterous marriage is a lawful marriage. We are not practicing truth. We are compounding iniquity upon iniquity. Cowards produce adulterers, who produce liars, who produce murderers, and so on and so on. Some of it is spiritual. Some of it is physical. All of it is unacceptable worship.

Because God hates our worship, we are losing everything. We are losing our churches, our children, our culture, our economy, our spiritual satisfaction, our power, and our authority. We are getting creamed, and I have not heard one credible argument for why. I hear only insightful diagnoses of symptoms and prognoses of the development of those symptoms, but I don't hear insightful diagnoses of the cause of the symptoms, or how to truly deal with those causes. The kingdom is under attack. It needs warriors who are smart and brave and holy. The kingdom of heaven suffers violence. It is time for violent men to take it back.

CHAPTER 5

NEW COVENANT VIOLENCE

SINCE THE CHURCH IS IN this place of ubiquitous unrepentant sin, what does it look like to follow Christ? The answer is to be violent. Violence solves problems. Otherwise why would the state be invested with the authority of the sword (Romans 13:4)? But I am not concerned with God's ministers of vengeance here. I am concerned with God's ministers of grace, which means I am advocating not physical violence but spiritual violence. The kingdom of heaven suffers violence, and violent men take it by force (Matthew 11:12).

Paul frequently employs martial language to describe the Christian life. He tells us that we wrestle not against flesh and blood but against the authorities, cosmic powers over the present darkness, and spiritual forces of evil in the heavenly places (Ephesians 6:12). And "though we walk in the flesh, we do not war after the flesh: For the weapons of our warfare are not carnal, but mighty through God to the pulling down of strong holds; Casting down imaginations, and every high thing that exalteth itself against the knowledge of God, and bringing into captivity every thought to the obedience of Christ; And having in a readiness to revenge all disobedience, when your obedience is fulfilled" (2 Corinthians 10:3–6). He tells his protégé, Timothy, to be "strong in the grace that is in Christ Jesus" and to "endure hardship as a good soldier of Jesus Christ. No one engaged in warfare entangles himself with the affairs of this life, that he may please him who enlisted him as a soldier" (2 Timothy 2:1–4). He also tells him to wage good warfare by the prophecies made about him (1 Timothy 1:18).

Paul suggests that the Church is a killing machine. He does this by employing what is most likely an aristeia in his letter to the Ephesians. An aristeia is a literary device in ancient Greek epic poetry. The general structure goes like this: the gods inspire a warrior, the warrior's armor is mentioned, and the warrior goes on a killing spree. We see this in the *Iliad* with several characters, most notably Achilles toward the end. This also occurs in the *Odyssey* when Odysseus slaughters his wife's suitors. It strongly appears that Paul employs an aristeia when writing to the Greek saints at Ephesus. He tells them to put on their combat gear because they are entering into battle (Ephesians 6:10–11). They would associate the inspiration of God in His Church and the mention of God's armor with the aristeia formula and, by implication, the subsequent killing spree against the spiritual enemies of God.

In the baptismal rite of Eastern Orthodox tradition, the person prepared for baptism, the catechumen, is asked, "Dost thou renounce Satan, and all his Angels, and all his works, and all his services, and all his pride?"[50] Schmemman goes on to explain the significance of the convert's baptism:

> The first act of the Christian life is a renunciation, a challenge. No one can be Christ's until he has, first, faced evil, and then become ready to *fight* it. How far is this spirit from the way in which we often proclaim, or to use a more modern term "sell" Christianity today! Is it not usually presented as a comfort, help, release from tensions, a reasonable investment of time, energy and money? "Religion" is almost invariably presented as salvation from something—fear, frustration, anxiety—but never as the salvation of man and the world. How could we then speak of "*fight*" when the very set-up of our churches must by definition, convey the idea of softness, comfort, peace? How can the Church use again the military language, which was its own in the first days, when it still thought of itself as *militia Christi?* One does not see very well where and how "fight" would fit into the weekly bulletin of a suburban parish, among all kinds of counseling sessions, bake sales, and "young adult" get togethers.

---

50 Alexander Schmemman, *For the Life of the World* (New York: St. Vladimir's Seminary Press, 1973), 71.

And yet it is, indeed, the necessary condition of the next and decisive step:

> It is difficult to convince a modern Christian that to be the life of the world, the Church must not "keep smiling" at the world, putting the "All Welcome" signs on the churches, and adjusting its language to that of the last best seller. The beginning of the Christian life—of the life in the Church—is humility, obedience, and discipline.[51]

It is true that life in Christ offers comfort and peace, but entering into the Promised Land does not come without wilderness wandering and the warfare of purging the enemies of God from the land. The problem with modern Christians is that they want the comfort and peace without the battle, without the violence. They think that salvation is the process of being teleported from Egypt to Canaan without any of the intermediate suffering and warfare. But salvation is just the end of one battle and the beginning of another. Salvation is crossing the Red Sea and drowning those Egyptian masters in the waters of baptism, and then beginning a life of suffering and violent warfare.

Jesus uses violent language when preaching on the seriousness of sin—plucking out eyes and chopping off hands—teaching us that we must rip out our hearts from our chests in order to be given new ones. Of course, this is all figurative language, but it is also *violent* language. He talks of our enemies being those of our own household. Enemies? Must we use that language? In the book of Revelation, Jesus violently renders judgment. And of course, there exists the famous temple cleansing by Christ, which most likely happened twice. Jesus, our master, demands violence from us and shows us how it's done, ultimately, by violently sacrificing His physical body for His body, which is His people.

The Lord's commands for us to be violent are first seen in the Noahic Covenant. Men were prohibited from avenging Abel for Cain's murder, but after the flood, God entrusts authority to men to act as avengers of blood.

---

51 Ibid., 71–72 (emphasis Schmemman's).

Simultaneously, the Lord also allows men to eat the meat of animals, which means they are now allowed to slaughter animals for food. The authority to kill murderers is paralleled with the authority to kill animals.[52] This kind of violence is delegated by God to men after the flood and also typifies ecclesiastical violence in the form of excommunication. God enacted both types of violence on Adam and Eve—they were excommunicated, and they also eventually literally died. These forms of judgment were given to men after the flood. As history advanced and men matured, God gave them more responsibility, like children growing up, and that responsibility entailed being violent.

To help structure the priority of violence to which Christians are obligated, I offer three categories: violence toward self, violence toward believers, and violence toward nonbelievers.

To be violent toward yourself means to put the sins of your life to death. If you are enslaved to sin, you cannot fight for the freedom of others. Paul says that we ought to put to death the deeds of the flesh by the Spirit (Romans 8:13) and that if we don't exercise this violence toward ourselves, we will die. He says to put to death the members on earth that are "fornication, uncleanness, passion, evil desire, and covetousness, which is idolatry" (Colossians 3:5). He goes on to say that God's wrath is coming to those who do not inflict this kind of violence on themselves. Being at peace with these sins indicates that you are a child of disobedience and you belong to the Old Man in Adam. When you repent, you renounce your fleshly self. You are declaring war on your sin. You are saying, "I am my enemy." You are announcing that you are no longer a passive man, being manipulated and enslaved to your sinful desires, but that you are now a human in Christ, who is a man of war (Exodus 15:3).

The conservative evangelical wing of the Church does, in general, a satisfactory job in preaching and practicing this aspect. There are hypocrites everywhere, but the conservative branch of the Church does at least preach and practice this. What we fail to preach and practice is violence toward believers.

---

52 James Jordan, "A Christian View of War," available at wordmp3.com.

Purge the Evil Person from Among You

Violence toward believers is the second category mentioned above. This is the most deficient category in the modern Church and is the primary reason why we have failed to take the land, to win the culture wars, and to keep our children from apostatizing, why we are being overrun by foreign hordes, and so forth. We are losers because we refuse to be violent toward believers. Here again it is not physical violence. It is spiritual violence that is commanded by Jesus and Paul.

In the Old Covenant, when someone was in sin, the law gave provisions for putting the sinner to death. In the New Covenant, whenever Jesus and Paul address unrepentant believers, they make explicit reference to these Old Covenant laws, but instead of stoning the sinner to death, the sinner is excommunicated. Excommunication is the New Covenant violence that we have abandoned.

Jesus instructs us to stop associating with someone who refuses to repent for his or her sins:

> Moreover if your brother sins against you, go and tell him his fault between you and him alone. If he hears you, you have gained your brother. But if he will not hear, take with you one or two more, that "by the mouth of two or three witnesses every word may be established." And if he refuses to hear them, tell it to the church. But if he refuses even to hear the church, let him be to you like a heathen and a tax collector. Assuredly, I say to you, whatever you bind on earth will be bound in heaven, and whatever you loose on earth will be loosed in heaven. Again I say to you that if two of you agree on earth concerning anything that they ask, it will be done for them by My Father in heaven. For where two or three are gathered together in My name, I am there in the midst of them. (Matthew 18:15–20)

Jesus first tells us to confront the sinner in private. I have witnessed far too many people in the Church who go straight to their pastors or some other authority instead of going to the individual who is in sin. This completely bypasses the first step Jesus commands. To go to your pastor or some kind of an ecclesiastical authority first reveals that either you are ignorant of Christ's commands or you are a coward who is afraid of confronting the person in private. Get violent, Christian! Harden up and get ready to be verbally beaten by someone who is hostile and impenitent, or get ready to slay death by saving that person's soul and covering a multitude of sins (James 5:20). Either way, get into the battle! But don't avoid the confrontation by abdicating responsibility to someone else. Lean into the confrontation. Don't run and tell. Confront and rebuke, and do so wisely. Some people may need only to be gently rebuked, others harshly.

Now, there may be times when circumstance doesn't allow or require this type of thing. We are not told whether Paul first confronted Peter in private when Peter threatened the gospel by withdrawing table fellowship from the gentiles. Paul rebuked him openly in front of everyone. A public sin may require a public rebuke. But the common denominator here is that Paul confronted Peter himself. He wasn't afraid to brawl, and Peter wasn't afraid to accept the beating.

The language Jesus uses for excommunication recalls Deuteronomic law, which prescribed stoning the sinner to death: "One witness shall not rise against a man concerning any iniquity or any sin that he commits; by the mouth of two or three witnesses the matter shall be established" (Deuteronomy 17:6, 19:15, and other similar verses). Jesus is saying that in order to sufficiently bring an accusation against someone, there must be two or three witnesses corroborating the accusation, just as the law requires. But in the New Covenant, someone may at this point repent of sin and be restored into the fellowship of believers, the Church, the Garden.

But if that person still refuses to repent, then the matter is to be brought publicly to the entire Church. And if the person still refuses to repent, according to the New Covenant violence, unlike the Old Covenant violence, which would put him to death, he is put to death via excommunication. This is what Jesus means when He says to treat them like heathens or tax collectors. Avoid them. Consider them unclean. Keep away from their fellowship.

This seems harsh to us, but notice the preference for mercy. They are not killed physically; they are killed spiritually. We have glimpses of this in the

Old Covenant too, but it comes to its fullness in the New. Adam and Eve are excommunicated from the garden as opposed to being immediately killed. Cain is not killed for his murder. King David is not put to death for his murder and adultery. The sodomites and prostitutes in Israel are excommunicated from the land under the reign of Asa.

Death would have been a just punishment for these crimes, and everyone in the human race does eventually die because of the sin of Adam. The temporal punishments for an individual's sin in the Old Covenant sometimes allowed for death, but as we see here, it wasn't always implemented, though different punishments were still enacted. However, Christ is saying that the law that justly could put to death sinners in the Old Covenant teaches us the seriousness of our sin, that it causes death, and that the wages of sin is death. But in the New Covenant, sinners are put to death by being ostracized, shunned, and excommunicated. Their lives are preserved for a time so that perhaps God may grant them repentance.

We see the fulfillment of the law from Old Covenant violence to New Covenant violence continue with Paul (1 Corinthians 5). He confronts the sins of believers in Corinth. He corrects a mistake that the Christians at Corinth made. He told them not to associate with immoral people, but he didn't mean immoral people of the world. That is an impossible thing to do. He meant that they should not associate with other Christians who are immoral. He tells them not even to eat dinner with someone who is a Christian and continues in sin. He tells them to "purge the evil person from among you" (1 Corinthians 5:13). Paul is quoting Deuteronomy here: "You must purge the evil from among you. All Israel will hear of it and be afraid" (Deuteronomy 21:21. See also Deuteronomy 13:5, 17:7, 17:12, 21:22–24, 22:21, and Judges 20:13). In the Deuteronomic context, this was a command to kill the sinner with stones, but in the New Covenant context, it's a command to kill the sinner with disassociation.

The violence of excommunication appears in varying degrees over a dozen times in the New Testament. We have already discussed two, Matthew 18:15–18 and some of 1 Corinthians 5. I will quote the rest here to further make the point and to also push against the idea (which I have frequently encountered) that it is a better plan to win people over with love rather than disassociation. This, of course, changes the definition of love and is actually the opposite of love. It assumes that disassociation is not loving. But it's always loving to obey Christ. Winning over your apostate Christian friends and family to Christ will not work if you are not obeying Christ in the first place.

All these quotes have contexts that deal with various sins, heresies, and people, but the essence of New Covenant violence, as I have described above, is present in all of them.

Paul to the Romans:

> Now I urge you, brethren, note those who cause divisions and offenses, contrary to the doctrine which you learned, and avoid them. (Romans 16:17)

Paul to the Corinthians:

> And you are puffed up, and have not mourned, that he who has done this deed might be taken away from among you. (1 Corinthians 5:2)

Paul to the Corinthians:

> Your glorying is not good. Do you not know that a little leaven leavens the whole lump? Therefore purge out the old leaven, that you may be a new lump, since you truly are unleavened. (1 Corinthians 5:6–7)

Paul to the Ephesians:

> But fornication and all uncleanness or covetousness, let it not even be named among you, as is fitting for saints…and have no fellowship with the unfruitful works of darkness, but rather expose them. (Ephesians 5:3, 5:11)

Paul to the Thessalonians:

> But we command you, brethren, in the name of our Lord Jesus Christ, that you withdraw from every brother who walks disorderly and not according to the tradition which he received from us. (2 Thessalonians 3:6)

Paul to the Thessalonians:

> And if anyone does not obey our word in this epistle, note that person and do not keep company with him, that he may be ashamed. (2 Thessalonians 3:14)

Paul to Timothy:

> Those who are sinning rebuke in the presence of all, that the rest also may fear. (1 Timothy 5:20)

Paul to Timothy:

> Having a form of godliness but denying its power. And from such people turn away! (2 Timothy 3:5, or in the New American Standard Version, "avoid such men")

Paul to Timothy:

> Men of corrupt minds and destitute of the truth, who suppose that godliness is a means of gain. From such withdraw yourself. (2 Timothy 6:5)

Paul to Titus:

> For there are many insubordinate...whose mouths must be stopped. (Titus 1:10–11)

Paul to Titus:

> Reject a divisive man after the first and second admonition. (Titus 3:10)

John to the Elect Lady and Her Children:

> If anyone comes to you and does not bring this doctrine, do not receive them into your house nor greet him; for he who greets him shares in his evil deeds. (2 John 10)

What the New Covenant arrangement does is both more gracious and more severe. It is more gracious because it gives people a chance to repent from their sins and be restored. That is the goal of excommunication, to be restored. New Covenant violence kills sinners in the hopes that they will resurrect. It is more severe in that a person who is excommunicated has been handed over to Satan (1 Corinthians 5:5; 1 Timothy 1:20). Those who trample underfoot the Spirit of grace will receive a more severe punishment than the punishments administered under the Mosaic Law (Hebrews 10:29).

THE SIN OF HAM

In Genesis 9, Noah sins, and Ham fails to restore his father properly. He fails to obey the first step in Jesus's commands we discussed above. He did not confront his father's sin in private. Ham discovers his father's nakedness, which is symbolic of sin, and instead of properly restoring his father with garments to cover his nakedness, he runs and tells his brothers. Shem and Japheth walk backward into the tent and cover their father without seeing his nakedness. Covering Noah with garments symbolizes the forgiveness of sin. It covers the sin, just as Christ's blood covers our sin, just as we are cloaked in His righteousness. Noah goes from a state of sin to a state of forgiveness.

When Noah wakes up, he does something remarkable. He curses Ham's son, Canaan! He doesn't curse Ham, who failed to properly confront his father's sin. How does that make sense? Ham's son is cursed because of Ham's sin. Ham escaped the curse, but his son did not. Canaan's children are to be expelled from the Promised Land. Much of the Old Testament surrounds the expulsion of the Canaanites. This all happened because Ham did not properly confront his father when he was in sin.

God is showing us that this is a big deal. He is saying that failing to do this correctly has horrific consequences. When you live your life associating with your family, friends, and church family without confronting them about their sins, you open yourself up to having your children cursed, just as Ham's child was cursed. I believe that this is seen in children literally dying, children leaving the faith, children of conservatives becoming homosexuals, and other various forms of walking away from the faith.

As discussed above, Jesus punished the church in Thyatira by cursing their children because they did not confront the false prophetess Jezebel. God promises that miscarriages will not occur when His people obey Him. Curses also come upon the people when they take the Lord's Supper while in sin. I believe all these curses are promised to go away if we would simply get violent with other Christians. Confront them in their sins. Excommunicate them when they refuse to repent. Avoid them when they obstinately remain in their sin. And comfort and reassure them when they do repent. Restore fellowship with them when they submit to the yoke of Christ.

This is the goal. But modern Christians want their fellowship the way they want their salvation: immediate and without difficulty. Confrontation. Violence. Excommunication. These things are all part of what is required in the community of believers. You cannot have a healthy Church body without them. And you cannot expect to disciple the nations successfully when you have failed to disciple the disciples first. "For what have I to do with judging those also who are outside? Do you not judge those who are inside? But those who are outside God judges" (1 Corinthians 5:13). Judgment begins at the house of the Lord, and when we do this correctly, the house of the Lord will begin to expand and conquer its enemies.

CONQUERING CANAAN IS CONQUERING THE WORLD

The third category is violence toward nonbelievers. This is the violence of evangelism, which manifests in conversions. In the Old Covenant, God's enemies were often killed. The Promised Land was taken through physical warfare. In the New Covenant, God's enemies are converted. The Promised Land is all the world, and it is taken through spiritual warfare. Conversion is conquering. Conversion is dying and resurrecting in Christ.

This idea becomes more evident when we reflect on the following comparisons. Three thousand men are killed when God gives His word (law) at Sinai (Exodus 32:28). Three thousand men are "pierced to the heart," killed, and resurrected in Christ (converted) when God gives His Holy Spirit and after Peter finishes delivering God's word to the hearers at Jerusalem during Pentecost (Acts 2:37, 2:41).

The structure of the book of Joshua is similar to the structure of the book of Acts with respect to the parallels between significant battles in Joshua and conversions in Acts.[53] In Joshua, the centrally located Jericho and Ai in the Promised Land are conquered (Joshua 6). In Acts, three thousand conversions occur at the centrally located Jerusalem in the Promised Land (Acts 2). In Joshua, the southern parts of the Promised Land, including Hebron and Gaza, are conquered (Joshua 10). In Acts, the Ethiopian eunuch is converted as he is travelling south toward Gaza (Acts 8). In Joshua, the northern territory, to include Hazor, is conquered (Joshua 11). In Acts, Cornelius, his family, and his friends are converted in the northern city of Caesarea (Acts 10).

Land beyond the literal Promised Land of Canaan is given to the tribes of Gad and Reuben and to the half tribe of Manasseh (Joshua 13). I believe this anticipates the conquering of the entire world, like a first fruit typifying what will happen everywhere eventually. In Acts, this is geographically seen when Paul, the Apostle to the gentiles, begins to convert and disciple believers in numerous cities outside of the literal Promised Land of Canaan (Acts 13–28). His energetic missionary journeys were the first major assault on the gentile

---

53 I have to credit James Jordan for bringing these parallels to my attention; however, I am unsure where I read or heard this from him.

world in conquering cities and men through conversion to the kingdom of Christ. This is what successful New Covenant violence looks like.

But the violence of converting men, families, and nations, of drowning the world in the waters of baptism, is successful only when the people of God have dealt New Covenant violence to themselves, their families, and their churches first. In other words, Christians will not be victorious in exercising dominion over the world, as we have been commanded to, until we judge ourselves rightly first.

THE SIN OF ACHAN

When Joshua and the Israelites entered into the Promised Land, they were obedient to the Lord, and the result was that they destroyed Jericho. They had total victory. Then they went on to attack the city of Ai, which did not have many people, and Israel was totally defeated.

What happened? One Israelite sinned. One! Achan stole things from Jericho. These things were off-limits to the Israelites. If we could speculate for a moment that Achan was like many Christians in the modern Church, he probably thought that because God is gracious, He would understand if he indulged a little bit. Why should he have to follow these legalistic restrictions? God isn't a legalist. Grace, grace, grace! He could ask for forgiveness later. This was not the case with Achan, and it is not the case with us.

Because Achan sinned, the rest of Israel, the rest of the Church, the other Christians he was living with, were unable to have victory. They were decisively defeated. They stood by and watched as a relatively few people in Ai defeated a three-thousand-man Israelite army. They stood by and watched as the Supreme Court handed down its Obergefell decision. They stood by and watched as Planned Parenthood sold murdered babies for profit. They stood by and watched as their congregations struggled with porn, homosexuality, and pedophilia. No victors. Just losers.

But Achan had a good pastor and elders. Joshua and the elders earnestly sought the Lord about why they were losing, something most pastors unfortunately just take as a normality for Christians, and God told them to stop praying and to get off their faces. He said, "Get up! Why do you lie thus on your face? Israel has sinned, and they have also transgressed My covenant which I commanded them" (Joshua 7:10–11). The obviousness of why they lost is spoken by God here in a tone that is almost exasperated at why Joshua was even asking. God goes on to explain further that if they do not deal with the sin in their church, they will continue to lose.

> For they have even taken some of the accursed things, and have both stolen and deceived; and they have also put it among their own stuff. Therefore the children of Israel could not stand before their enemies, but turned their backs before their enemies, because they have become doomed to destruction. Neither will I be with you anymore, unless you destroy the accursed from among you. Get up, sanctify the people, and say, "Sanctify yourselves for tomorrow, because thus says the Lord God of Israel: 'There is an accursed thing in your midst, O Israel; you cannot stand before your enemies until you take away the accursed thing from among you.'" (Joshua 7:11–13)

You cannot stand before your enemies until you take away the accursed thing from among you. This is what God is saying of us too. We have prayer meeting after prayer meeting, begging God for reformation, revival, and restoration. If we would simply make the connection that we are losers because we are unrepentant sinners, we would make tremendous strides toward victory. But as it is, we point to things that aren't really the main sins or are not as egregious as the adultery we affirm in divorce and remarriage. Instead, we say we need to think more covenantally or be louder with our condemnation of abortion or homosexuality, or we formulate things like the Benedict Option, where we learn how to give up our dominion mandate. We tell ourselves that this isn't really our home and that maybe if persecution came, we would be the better for it.

But God is saying to his people, "Get up! Stop praying, and start doing! You cowards have sinned and tolerated sin. That's why the world is mopping the floor with you. Now go and kill the sinners in your midst. Purge the evil people from among you. Stop whining, and start killing." This is what the Holy Spirit is speaking to the Church. He is telling us to excommunicate those who are practicing adultery through divorce and remarriage if they do not repent and, especially, to excommunicate those leaders who have perpetuated the sin if they are not repentant. When the rest of Israel sees this happen, they will be compliant. They will fear when they see Christians slaughtering their brothers and sisters in sin.

Achan wasn't facilitated and affirmed in his sin as the Achans among us are. Our situation is more like Joshua assisting Achan in stealing things from Jericho, holding a public ceremony for all Israel to see Achan dedicate himself to the stolen things, and speaking comforting words to Achan like, "As long as you honor God with your stolen things, God accepts you. Just as God stole us out of Egypt, Achan, you have stolen these things out of Jericho. What you have done reflects the character of God. Good job! Everyone else, go and do likewise!"

Our pastors say, "As long as you glorify God with your stolen wife, God will accept you. Just as Ruth was alone and needed someone to redeem her, this woman who was alone after her divorce needed someone like you to come along and be her Boaz! You are reflecting the character of God in loving this woman and adopting her children. You are being Christ to her. Everyone else, go and do likewise!" But just as Joshua did not approve of what Achan did, our pastors should not approve of what our friends and family are doing when they steal other peoples' wives and husbands and when they forsake the legitimate covenants they made with their true wives and husbands.

Achan's pastor and church responded with appropriate violence toward him for his sin. They destroyed not only Achan but everything he owned, from his children to his iPhone. They destroyed it all: "So all Israel stoned him with stones; and they burned them with fire after they had stoned them with stones. Then they raised over him a great heap of stones, still there to this day. So the Lord turned from the fierceness of His anger" (Joshua 7:25–26). Everyone that was part of his church took part in the punishment of his sin. They all had to throw stones. In New Covenant violence, everyone must participate in the punishment of sinners by not associating with them. Everyone takes part in the excommunication. The seriousness of the sin is reflected in the seriousness of the punishment.

Notice that once the sin was dealt with, once the violence against the sin occurred, God relented from His anger. His punishment seems severe to us modern Americans, who don't even like to spank our bratty kids. But because the sin was dealt with adequately, God then directed Joshua and Israel to give Ai another go. He essentially said, "You're going to win. I've already given you victory." And Joshua and Israel went, and they destroyed their enemies at Ai and Ai itself.

These things were written as an example for us so that we can learn from them. Victory is dependent on the people of God obeying Him and dealing with unrepentant sin in the Church. If we are to be victorious in our warfare, we must understand this.

A Sin Shish Kebab

Consider another example—Phinehas. In Numbers 25, the Israelites want to have sex with Moabite and Midianite women. In order to do so, they needed to worship the women's gods, which they did. Then God tells Moses to hang all the offenders.

> So Moses said to the judges of Israel, "Every one of you kill his men who were joined to Baal of Peor." And indeed, one of the children of Israel came and presented to his brethren a Midianite woman in the sight of Moses and in the sight of all the congregation of the children of Israel, who were weeping at the door of the tabernacle of meeting. Now when Phinehas the son of Eleazar, the son of Aaron the priest, saw it, he rose from among the congregation and took a javelin in his hand; and he went after the man of Israel into the tent and thrust both of them through, the man of Israel, and the woman through her body. So the plague was stopped among the children of Israel. (Numbers 25:5–8)

A nice Christian man, who probably had great manners, presented the Midianite woman to his buddy in front of the entire church. Notice that everyone, including the pastor, Moses, was just standing around doing nothing but crying. But when Phinehas saw the sin taking place, he decided to get violent. He took a spear and made a sinner shish kebab with it. And what happened immediately after he did this? The plague stopped. The violence demanded by the Lord was obeyed, and the deleterious effects of sin dissipated.

We need more men in the Church to be like Phinehas, instead of the rest of Israel, who are standing around weeping over the sin that is being committed in the Church. We have plenty of men just sulking about our sin and doing nothing about it. Consider the commendatory language God uses of Phinehas:

> Phinehas the son of Eleazar, the son of Aaron the priest, has turned back My wrath from the children of Israel, because he was zealous with My zeal among them, so that I did not consume the children of Israel in My zeal. Therefore say, "Behold, I give to him My covenant of peace; and it shall be to him and his descendants after him a covenant of an everlasting priesthood, because he was zealous for his God, and made atonement for the children of Israel." (Numbers 23:11–13)

Phinehas is also commended by the Psalmist:

> They joined themselves also to Baal of Peor,
> And ate sacrifices made to the dead.
> Thus they provoked Him to anger with their deeds,
> And the plague broke out among them.
> Then Phinehas stood up and intervened,
> And the plague was stopped.
> And that was accounted to him for righteousness
> To all generations forevermore. (Psalm 106:28–31)

God was so pleased with Phinehas's zealousness that He gave His covenant of peace and everlasting priesthood not only to Phinehas but also to his descendants after him. This is the opposite of the sin of Ham. Phinehas correctly dealt with the sin in his (church) family, and his children were blessed because of it, instead of cursed. His zealous violence eradicated the plague on the Church. And the Psalmist says that his zealous violence was accounted to him for righteousness to all generations forevermore.

How many think of Phinehas when they think of justification? The Bible tells us he was justified by these actions; what he did was accounted to him for righteousness. This is the same language used of Abraham about believing in God's promises, which Paul recalls in Romans 4 when discussing justification. Phinehas believed that God cursed those who transgressed His covenant and blessed those who obeyed it, and that belief became apparent when he stood up and intervened. May it be in our day as well. May there be an army of those who have the faith of Phinehas to act violently toward believers when the rest of the Church is standing around and doing nothing but crying.

BENJAMIN IS A RAVENOUS WOLF, AND HE MUST BE PUNISHED

When the first two categories of New Covenant violence are adequately practiced, violence toward self and believers, the result will be success in the third, violence toward nonbelievers. Men will be converted, which, in turn, becomes families that are converted, which, in turn, becomes cultures that are converted, which, in turn, becomes nations and their rulers that are converted. Properly ordered New Covenant violence will manifest in a vibrant Christian culture, scientific advancement, poetic and artistic excellence, free societies, and limited governments. So when we see that we are losing these things, we should inquire of the Lord, as Joshua did when he was unsuccessful in conquering Ai the first time.

And when we inquire of the Lord, His Holy Spirit will affirm what His Son has affirmed—that divorce and remarriage is adultery and as long as we tolerate it among the people of God, He will continue to hand our nation, culture, and families over to liberals, Muslims, atheists, sodomites, feminists and so forth. Jesus affirms this immediately after his teaching on excommunication: "Truly, I say to you, whatever you bind on earth shall be bound in heaven, and whatever you loose on earth shall be loosed in heaven" (Matthew 18:18). We will continue to lose if we do not bind this and if we do not go to war against this.

If you are convinced that it is necessary to go to war against this gross perverseness, you will encounter heavy resistance, and that resistance will come from other believers who are dedicated to defending this sexual immorality. They are like the Benjamites who raped and murdered the concubine in Judges 19 and 20. When the rest of Israel heard what their brother Benjamin had done, they decided to go to war against him, and it was a fierce and bloody civil war.

This is what I suspect the Church is going to look like in the coming years. You will begin to see increased awareness of the rape and murder of the gospel through the pernicious practice of adulterous marriage, and this awareness will manifest in Christians filled with the Spirit of God who are willing to go to war. These Christians are part of the tribe of modern-day Judah—the faithful remnant. "Then the children of Israel arose and went up to the house of God to inquire of God. They said, 'Which of us shall go up first to battle against the children of Benjamin?' The Lord said, 'Judah first!'" (Judges 20:18). This is already happening. I have witnessed the beginning skirmishes. I have seen the Jezebel spirit in the lives of otherwise sweet Christian women and nice Christian men who oppose the faithful remnant. I have seen the horrified and disdainful looks in their faces, these modern Benjamites who have no shame in what they are practicing and protecting. These present-day Benjamites are already reacting the same way the Benjamites did when the rest of Israel confronted their sin:

> Then the tribes of Israel sent men through all the tribe of Benjamin, saying, "What is this wickedness that has occurred among you? Now therefore, deliver up the men, the perverted men who are in Gibeah, that we may put them to death and remove the evil from Israel!" But the children of Benjamin would not listen to the voice of their brethren, the children of Israel. Instead, the children of Benjamin gathered together from their cities to Gibeah, to go to battle against the children of Israel. And from their cities at that time the children of Benjamin numbered twenty-six thousand men who drew the sword, besides the inhabitants of Gibeah, who numbered seven hundred select men. Among all this people were seven hundred select men who were left-handed; every one could sling a stone at a hair's breadth and not miss. Now besides Benjamin, the men of Israel numbered four hundred thousand men who drew the sword; all of these were men of war. (Judges 20:12–17)

The Benjamites were given the chance to exercise proper discipline of the perverted people in their midst, but they refused and chose, rather, to fight against the rest of Israel. This is a portrait of our current situation. Those of us in the tribe of Judah, and soon to be the rest of Israel, have warned the Church to exercise proper discipline of their perverted people—those who are divorced and remarried—but they refuse.

The Benjamites among us are men of valor (Judges 20:44, 20:46). This is similar to respectable people of God who are on the wrong side of this war. In my experience, they are mostly Reformed evangelicals, but of course they can also be those in other Christian circles. They are good in battle. They are highly educated. They know how to argue. They aren't afraid to fight for their tribes, even if their tribes are committing filthy whoredom.

A great Reformed pastor from Brooklyn once said, "The problem with Reformed people is that they have no abiding interest in reforming." They are like the seven hundred select men who were left handed. They can sling a stone at a hair's breadth and not miss. They are like David Instone-Brewer, Craig Keener, Jay Adams, Ray Sutton, Greg Bahnsen, Andrew Luck, Martin Bucer, John Milton, and every other man who is incredibly gifted and intelligent but is fighting on the wrong side of this issue. They can write brilliant defenses of adulterous marriages. Their arguments are precise and accurate in many ways, but they are defending the rape and murder of the Levite's concubine. They are defending sin, and they will ultimately be defeated.

However, they will not be defeated easily. Israel attacked the Benjamites three times before they were successful, and Israel suffered heavy casualties. They lost 22,000 men in the first battle, 18,000 men in the second, but only 30 in the third (Judges 20:21, 25, 31, 39). Israel finally won in the third battle, and it was a decisive victory. The Benjamite army numbered 26,000 men (Judges 20:15), and the number of Benjamites killed in the third battle numbered 25,100 (Judges 20:35). Their remaining army was 900 men. The Israelites resolved not to totally destroy the Benjamites and came up with a plan to restore them (Judges 21:17–24).

This demonstrates to us that every part of the body of Christ is needed. We can't simply say of the Benjamites, "We don't need them, because they wanted to protect wicked men." They must be punished, but they also must be restored, for all our benefit. From the restored tribe of Benjamin arises the Apostle Paul. So when we go to war with Benjamin now, we need to win decisively but also remember that the goal is not annihilation but restoration and for them to give the Church more Pauls.

The final thing in this episode worth mentioning is the reluctance of all the children of Israel to fight their brother Benjamin. All the other tribes of Israel agree that Benjamin must be punished for this sin (Judges 20:10–11). But Israel gives the Benjamites a chance to offer up the offenders so that they may be killed, instead of going immediately to war with them. The Benjamites choose to defend the sinners in their tribe by going to war instead.

After the first battle, the Israelites weep and inquire of the Lord whether they should continue battling with their brother Benjamin (Judges 20:23). God tells them to continue fighting. After the second battle, they weep, fast, offer burnt and peace offerings, and inquire again to the Lord whether they should "go out to battle against the children of my brother Benjamin, or shall I cease?" (Judges 20:26). In both instances, the Israelites were reluctant to continue fighting. Perhaps this was because they were losing so many men, but I do not think this is the whole story. I believe they were heartbroken over having to fight their brother. In both prayers to God, they refer to the Benjamites as the "children of my brother Benjamin." I believe it brought true grief to them that they had to war with their youngest brother.

I believe the text warrants this reading, and it also resonates with me on a personal level. I have spent about ten years doing this. I have gone to war with my brothers who want to defend the sinners in their tribe, and I have wept often over it because I love my brothers. I have gone on one-day, two-day, three-day, week-long, and month-long water-only fasts, asking the Lord what I should do: "Lord, am I to go to battle with my brother Benjamin?" And I am always told to continue fighting. It is something I wouldn't have chosen for myself, but it is what God requires if I desire to be faithful. It is what God requires if we are to stop the plague on the Church. It is what God requires if we are to be victorious in warfare. It is what God requires if we are to have reformation and revival.

CHAPTER 6

THE CHAINSAW REVIVAL

———

IN THE MIDST OF OUR cultural collapse, abortion on demand, pornography addiction, institutionalization of sodomite marriages, and the practice of divorce and remarriage, we are in need of a chainsaw revival. A chainsaw revival is what happened in Judges 6 and 7. These chapters serve as a type of how-to guide to reformation. Gideon took a chainsaw to the sinful worship in his church, and he was given subsequent victory in the culture wars. This story also typifies all three categories of New Covenant violence that I described in the previous chapter. It is not simply enough to pray for reformation. We must first submit ourselves, our families, our churches, and our culture to the word of God. As you will see, we must become lumberjacks. We must become like Gideon.

THE MIDIANITE TYRANNY OF THE AUTHORITARIAN LEFT

Gideon's actions taken against the Midianites[54] in chapter 7 seem to be more popularly known than some of the actions taken in chapter 6. But I am convinced that the victory in chapter 7 could not have happened without the chainsaw revival in chapter 6.

First consider Israel's relationship to Midian. We are told, "The Israelites did evil in the eyes of the Lord, and for seven years he gave them into the hands of the Midianites" (Judges 6:1). Midian was the son of Abraham's second

---

54 Midianites in this section refers to Midianites, Amalekites, and people of the East.

wife, Keturah. They were closely associated with the Ishmaelites (Genesis 37—Joseph's brothers sell him to the Midianites/Ishmaelites). They were also the Midianites from the East, which indicates they were a branch of Midian that was allied with Moab (Numbers 22:4–7). Moab was the offspring of Lot's incest with his daughters—signifying unbelief and sexual immorality.

What's interesting about this is that when Abraham is about to die, he gives "all that he had to Isaac," and he sends all his other sons to the East (Genesis 25:5–6). Later, in Numbers, the Midianites are not in the East. They are in the land that was given to Isaac, and when Israel was conquering the Promised Land, we are told the Israelites virtually destroyed them (Numbers 31:7). What we have in Judges 6 is the return of an enemy that had been previously beaten but not entirely destroyed. This enemy, Midian, was taking the inheritance that was not its to receive. Yet it was the Lord who had given the Israelites over to Midianite rule.

Israel's sin had brought them back into a type of Egypt. Israel had been promised the land of Canaan, a type of redemption for them from the bondage of Egypt. Yet we are told "because the power of Midian was so oppressive, the Israelites prepared shelters for themselves in mountain clefts, caves and strongholds" (Judges 6:2). God's people made prisons for themselves. They became slaves. They returned to Egypt. They worked, and the fruits of their labor were taken from them.

This is the nature of sin and a reversal of the nature of redemption: "I have given you a land for which you did not labor, and cities which you did not build, and you dwell in them; you eat of the vineyards and olive groves which you did not plant" (Joshua 24:13). Israel reaped what other people had sown when they entered the Promised Land and were obedient. But now Midianites, Amalekites, and people of the East would reap what Israel had sown—a complete reversal.

Then they would encamp against them and destroy the produce of the earth as far as Gaza, and leave no sustenance for Israel, neither sheep nor ox nor donkey. For they would come up with their livestock and their tents, coming in as numerous as locusts; both they and their camels were without number; and they would enter the land to destroy it. So Israel was greatly impoverished because of the Midianites, and the children of Israel cried out to the Lord. (Judges 6:4–6)

Israel is "impoverished" or "made low" (English Standard Version), which is the opposite of the promise given to Abraham: "And he brought him outside and said, 'Look toward heaven, and number the stars, if you are able to number them.' Then he said to him, 'So shall your offspring be'" (Genesis 15:5). This promise was to come through Isaac's children, but now the children of Midian were "coming in as numerous as locusts; both they and their camels were without number" (Judges 6:5). This is a complete reversal. None of the other stories in Judges draws so much attention to the type of oppression Israel experienced. Several centuries later, Isaiah references the Midianite oppression (Isaiah 9:4).

This is not unlike what the Church in America is experiencing now to some degree and the Church in Europe is experiencing in an almost-identical sense. The enemy is like locusts. They run the media, the arts, the government, the schools, how we speak, and so on. We sow the word through preaching and evangelizing, and we are pillaged by spiritual enemies, so we are unable to reap plentiful harvest. We are hiding in dens, caves, and strongholds and figuring out how to make the best of our subjugation (e.g., the Benedict Option). Like Israel, at this time, we are impoverished and made low, but this is not what God wants His Church to look like. This is what an impotent Church looks like, unable to inherit what the Lord has promised us: the world.

Europe is seeing this happen in almost the exact same way we read about in Judges 6. Europe is experiencing countless numbers of so-called refugees, migrant workers, and so on, who have no desire to assimilate into Western culture, who have brought remarkably increased levels of crime and rape. They are literally depleting the resources of European countries like Sweden and Germany by living off government-subsidized housing, food, and medical care. Apostate Christian Europe is being raped by Midianites, and America is starting to see the beginnings of this kind of judgment as well, and it will only increase unless we see a chainsaw revival. There are Christian men and women who are regularly crying out to God for revival, just as Israel did (verse 6). The Lord heard them as He hears us and answered them as He is answering us.

The Prophet, the Covenant, the Commissioning

How does the Lord answer Israel? How does the Lord grant them deliverance? Does He give them strong military leaders? Does He give them a political statesman like Winston Churchill? Does He give them immediate reprieve from the Midianites? No. Not yet. He sends a prophet. This prophet is sent to remind the people of their covenantal obligations to the Lord, to remember that God saved them and to obey the law (Judges 6:8–10). He reminds the Israelites of God's saving actions. He reminds them that these saving actions show that God is truly God. He then reminds them not to fear the gods of the Amalekites. Calamity, misfortune, and oppression are happening among God's people, and when they call for help, God sends them a prophet exhorting them to repent. Their disobedience brought about their misery.

The Midianites were not the ones to blame; the Israelites were. The homosexuals are not the ones to blame; the Church is. The liberals are not the ones to blame; the Church is. The feminists are not the ones to blame; the Church is. This is how God's covenant works. Everything has to do with God's covenant.

The Church doesn't like the idea that when bad things happen, it's because of sin. I'm not arguing that this is the case in every situation. Job was a righteous man who had everything taken away from him (though he was given more in his restoration than what he initially had). The tower of Siloam fell on the eighteen, who were no worse sinners than anyone else in Galilee (Luke 13). The apostles were beaten by the Sanhedrin. And Jesus, the perfect man, was crucified. So yes, Scripture teaches that bad things happen to the righteous.

But Scripture also teaches that bad things happen to sinners. The ground swallowed up Korah and everyone associated with his rebellion (Numbers 16:32, 26:10). Achan and his entire family were destroyed because of his sin, and Israel lost a battle at Ai because of it. Ananias and Sapphira drop dead immediately after lying to the Holy Spirit (Acts 5:1–11). The covenant God made with Israel stipulated blessings for obedience and curses for disobedience

(Deuteronomy 27–30). And here in the time of Gideon, Israel is cursed because of their disobedience. The Bible teaches both things to be true. And so we must affirm both to be true and speak with wisdom or not speak at all when discerning the reasons for tragedy. Peter summarizes it well: "For the eyes of the Lord are on the righteous, and His ears are open to their prayers; but the face of the Lord is against those who do evil. And who is he who will harm you if you become followers of what is good? But even if you should suffer for righteousness' sake, you are blessed" (1 Peter 3:12-14).

Despite the prophet telling the Israelites that they are not obeying the Lord (inferring that they need to repent in order for the oppression to yield), Gideon only partially understands why Israel is losing, which is remarkable because we are doing the same thing. He doesn't fully understand the Obergefell decision. He doesn't fully understand why feminists and cultural Marxists are running our institutions of higher education. He doesn't fully understand why the leaven of homosexuality is leavening all society. This partial understanding is revealed by the question Gideon asks to an angel of the Lord who appears to him: "O my lord, if the Lord is with us, why then has all this happened to us? And where are all His miracles which our fathers told us about, saying, 'Did not the Lord bring up from Egypt?' But now the Lord has forsaken us and delivered us into the hands of the Midianites" (Judges 6:13).

Gideon correctly recalls what God had done for them, but he doesn't recognize the false worship that Israel is engaged in. He doesn't see the connection between their disobedience and the cultural collapse in Israel. Again, this is exactly the partial understanding that pervades the Church. We understand that God is great and He does mighty things and delivers His people, but we are totally clueless when it comes to *why* we are seeing the suppression of Christianity and the impotence of its endeavors.

Gideon asks, "Where's the power? Where's the deliverance? Where is God at?" But the angel of the Lord does not give a direct reply. Instead he commissions Gideon to take back the land from the Midianites. He says, "Go in this might of yours and save Israel from the hand of Midian; do not I send you?" (Judges 6:14). In verse 16, he says, "But I will be with you, and you shall strike the Midianites as one man."

This phrase, "I will be with you," anticipates the Great Commission, by which Jesus commissions Christian soldiers to go into the battle for the world—which is the new inheritance, the New Covenant's Promised Land. Just as the Lord assures Gideon of His presence with him in battle, the Lord assures His warrior-disciples, "And surely I am with you always to the end of the age" (Matthew 28:20).

Gideon then offers an acceptable sacrifice to the angel of the Lord, which symbolizes Gideon's acceptable righteousness before the Lord. This is important as it evidences the first category of New Covenant violence in Gideon (even though this is still in the Old Covenant). He is violent toward himself. He is in warfare with the sins of his own flesh. His heart is upright before the Lord.

This also indicates that Gideon truly was a "mighty man of valor" as the angel of the Lord said he was. The angel of the Lord was not saying this jokingly, as some expositors have suggested. Just because Gideon was threshing in the winepress as opposed to the open field does not mean he was a coward; it means he was smart. He was doing the only thing he could to keep food for his household from being destroyed by the Midianites. And whatever criticisms expositors may levy against Gideon for how he acted in all subsequent events, at least Gideon actually did *something*!

Last it's important to note that God is pleased to use whomever He wishes to use, and often He uses unlikely candidates. Gideon was least in his house and not highly esteemed in Israel. He was not a Levite. His commissioning was not done officially in public by the Levitical presbytery. He did not receive proper training in Greek and Hebrew. He was not formally trained at a seminary, but he did offer sacrifices that were acceptable to the Lord, which is a testament to his character. You can have all the formal training in the world, but if your heart is not right before God, your sacrifice of worship will not be acceptable. Gideon's was.

DESTROYING THE SINS OF THE FATHER: LOVE, FEAR, AND LUNACY

What happens next? Does the Lord tell Gideon to immediately start recruiting an army to take out the Midianites? Does He tell him to spy on the

Midianites and assess their weaknesses? Does He tell him to execute the third category of New Covenant violence—violence toward nonbelievers? No, He tells him to execute the second category of New Covenant violence—violence toward believers. The Lord tells Gideon,

> Take your father's bull, and the second bull seven years old, and pull down the altar of Baal that your father has, and cut down the Asherah that is beside it and build an altar to the Lord your God on the top of the stronghold here, with stones laid in due order. Then take the second bull and offer it as a burnt offering with the wood of the Asherah that you shall cut down. (Judges 6:25–26)

This is the turning point. This is the most important event in Gideon's story as it pertains to our day. The Lord tells Gideon to take out the Midianites, but the first thing he is commanded to do is to tear down the Baal and Asherah in his father's house. God tells him to confront the sin in his family and his church. Had he refused to go to war with his family and his church, he wouldn't have gone to war against Midian, or he would not have been successful against Midian if he had.

Gideon was successful because he was not guilty of the sin of Ham. Battling the Midianites meant reclaiming the land that was promised to Israel, the land of Canaan. Canaan was Noah's grandson who was cursed because of Ham's failure to confront his father's sin correctly. As described in the previous chapter, Ham failed to properly confront his father's sin. He failed to restore his father. It was Shem and Japheth who walked backward into the tent so as not see their father's nakedness and covered him. Ham went and told his brothers and abdicated his responsibility to cover his father's nakedness himself first (he violated Matthew 18:15–17). Noah then cursed Ham's son Canaan because of this. Canaan, the person and the land, is strongly associated with the detrimental consequences of not properly confronting sin in your family. The same principles are in play with Gideon and his father. Gideon must confront his father's sin of Baal and Asherah worship.

Baal-berith means "lord, master, or possessor of the covenant." The lord of the covenant is the god of Baal worship (Judges 8:33). El-Berith, which means "god of the covenant," is mentioned in reference to a pagan god a few chapters later (Judges 9:46). These descriptions of false gods and false worship are remarkably similar to the names of the True God of Israel. Jehovah God is also God of the Covenant. Jehovah God is also referred to as Baal. In Hosea, he gets rid of this name, possibly because it's too similar to the name used by the god of false worship, but also because it marks a progression from master to husband—a more intimate name, which I believe anticipates the intimacy of God with his people in the New Covenant. The similarities of Baal worship and Jehovah worship are noted by Matthew Henry. He says that Baal's worshipers probably joined with him in covenant in imitation of Israel's covenanting with God.[55]

There isn't much description of Asherah or the Asherah poles in Scripture. Much of what we know about the worship of other nations outside of Israel comes from extrabiblical sources. Archaeological discoveries indicate that Asherah was considered a consort to Yahweh and that she was a fertility goddess. These discoveries include wooden figurines of a naked woman holding out large breasts, indicating promised vitality, life, and fertility.[56] There also seems to be indication that she was worshiped through sexual rituals (1 Kings 14:23–24).

I highlight these things to demonstrate that false worship can have a superficial similarity to true worship and that good things like vitality, life, fertility, and sex (all good things) can be used in unlawful worship. Some can worship God through their lawful marriages, and God will accept it as true worship, but others can say they are worshiping God through their unlawful marriages, and God will not accept it, because it is false worship. It is the worship of another god. The people of God in Gideon's family and church retained a form of godliness. They were still religious. They still went

---

55 Matthew Henry's Commentary on Judges 8:29-35 available at biblegateway.com.

56 Tully, E. (2016). Asherah. In J. D. Barry, D. Bomar, D. R. Brown, R. Klippenstein, D. Mangum, C. Sinclair Wolcott, W. Widder (Eds.), *The Lexham Bible Dictionary*. Bellingham, WA: Lexham Press.

to church on Sunday. They continued to make covenants, but with another god. Their worship consisted of immoral covenant making, just like divorce and remarriage—and God told Gideon to hack it down and burn it. Take a chainsaw to it! No reformation without chainsaws.

And that's exactly what Gideon did. Gideon tore down his father's altar (Judges 6:27). Not only did Gideon take a chainsaw to the Baal and the Asherah grove, not only did he essentially force his father to stop worshiping improperly, but the change of worship was costly to his father. Gideon took some of his father's livestock and sacrificed it. I bring this up because it's a detail that doesn't seem to make sense. Gideon sacrificed his father's livestock. His faithfulness was costly to his family. Deliverance is costly. When Jesus delivers the towns that were terrorized by the demoniac, it cost them some of their economic livelihood. The demons were cast into the pigs, which then committed suicide. Deliverance didn't come without a cost, without sacrifice, or without bloodshed.

Let me note here that it wasn't enough for Gideon to simply disapprove of his father's sin. It wasn't enough to simply "love" his father into taking down the Baal and Asherah poles. He couldn't just "love" his father into the kingdom in the way that evangelicals have defined love. Being nice, friendly, and diplomatic was not what Gideon needed to do. He needed to violently destroy the false worship himself. That is what true love looks like.

Augustine might describe this act of Gideon as properly ordered love. He placed his love for God over his love for family, which is what all Christians must do. Jesus says, "Whoever loves father or mother more than me is not worthy of me, and whoever loves son or daughter more than me is not worthy of me" (Matthew 10:37). Focus on the Family is a terrible name for a Christian organization. Focus on the family, and the family dies. Here, Gideon focuses on God. He loves God first and foremost, and he saves his family ultimately because of it.

In one of his letters, C. S. Lewis writes,

When I have learnt to love God better than my earthly dearest, I shall love my earthly dearest better than I do now. Insofar as I learn to love my earthly dearest at the expense of God and instead of God, I shall be moving towards the state in which I shall not love my earthly dearest at all. When first things are put first, second things are not suppressed, but increased.[57]

In placing God first, Gideon faced the possibility of losing his entire earthly family, but he would have gained a greater family—those who do the will of the Father, who have the faith of Abraham, and who are more numerous than the stars in the sky and sands of the seashore. When Jesus is told that His mother is looking for Him, He points to His disciples and says, "Those who do the will of my father in heaven are my mother, my brother, and my sister" (Matthew 12:50). Our family is a spiritual one first, which makes our blood family secondary.

Our problem is that we think we are loving our families more by allowing them to continue in sin, by rationalizing away their sin of unlawful marriage, but this is not love. It is its opposite—hate.

Gideon not only demonstrated love, he also demonstrated courage, but he was not without fear. He feared his family and the men of the city, so he confronted the sin stealthily (Judges 6:27). He tore down his father's Baal in the middle of the night.

Confronting sin is not an easy thing to do. Rebuking improper worship can be frightening. It can be like trying to take the ring away from Gollum. My precious! The sin of God's chosen people, the Church, was so precious to them that they wanted to kill Gideon for taking it away from them: "Bring Gideon out so that he may die" (Judges 6:30). Their love for breaking the commandments of God was so entrenched that they were willing to slit Gideon's throat.

This is also what is happening in the Church now, except we don't kill each other physically. We haven't reached that point. But the people of God *love* their adulterous marriages. They love their friends and family who are in adulterous marriages more than they love God. They love the social life they have built up, which requires them to make peace with this sin. And so they

---

57 C. S. Lewis, *The Collected Letters of C. S. Lewis, Volume lll: Narnia, Cambridge, and Joy 1950-1963* (Harper Collins: New York, 2007), 247.

often become hostile and defensive toward anyone who threatens to take that away from them. Do it anyway. Take it away from them. Take a chainsaw to their covenant-breaking whoredom. Burn their filthy rebellion to the ground.

Gideon didn't know what was going to happen after he dealt with his father's sin. He was simply being obedient. He could have died, and that would have been OK. He could have been ostracized by his family and by his church. He could have ruined his relationship with his father for the rest of his life. He wasn't being obedient because he knew exactly what was going to happen. He didn't know how it would unfold. He was simply obedient and wasn't paralyzed by trying to figure out what was going to happen. There was no guarantee that things would pan out the way he hoped. He knew only that God promised to be with him and that God told him to confront the sin. By faith, Gideon did this (Hebrews 11:32). This is what it is to have faith.

When a man places trust in God, he frequently looks like a lunatic to spectators. What did the world think of Noah as he built the ark? What was Sarah thinking when Abraham woke up early to sacrifice Isaac? What were David's brothers thinking when David went to fight Goliath without a sword or armor? What were Gideon's servants thinking when he told them his plan to take a chainsaw to the Baals and Asherahs? What was Gideon himself thinking? "God told us to do this, but I know everyone in the church is going to be outraged with me. They might even kill me." Gideon didn't know what would happen, but he knew it didn't matter as much as being obedient to the Lord did. In his commentary on Judges 6, Matthew Henry says, "Let us do our duty and trust God with our safety."[58]

Many of the dissenters of the traditional view of marriage do not think this way. They want to preserve their safety, their friendships, their families, their social lives, and their kingdoms and figure out a way to get God to fit in. However, if presented with the ultimatum "Renounce Christ or die," I don't doubt that many Christians would choose death. But when presented with the ultimatum "Renounce Christ or your social life will die," many Christians renounce Christ in order to keep their social lives. In some ways, it is more

---

58 Matthew Henry Commentary on Judges 6 available at biblegateway.com.

terrifying to face the consequences of renouncing our friends, family, and churches for the sake of Christ than it is to simply die a physical death for the sake of Christ. If we are going to have reformation, we must be more like Gideon in trusting God with the consequences of our obedience.

Gideon could have been a martyr for the faith, and that would have been glorious. But God had further plans for Gideon, and so the miraculous occurred. The last person you would expect to defend Gideon was his father, yet it was his father who came to his defense and saved him. The very man whose precious idols Gideon destroyed and whose livestock he slaughtered was the man who came to his defense. "But Joash said to all who stood against him, 'Will you contend for Baal? Or will you save him? Whoever contends for him shall be put to death by morning. If he is a god, let him contend for himself, because his altar has been broken down'" (Judges 6:31). The looming sentence of death took a radical reversal. Gideon, who was contending for God, was facing a death squad by the contenders of Baal. But Gideon's father reversed this by saving the life of the contender of God and putting to death the contenders of Baal.

After this pivotal event, the Midianites began to mobilize, maybe because they heard what Gideon had done but more likely because it was harvest time. We know this because Gideon was threshing the wheat in the winepress at the beginning of the passage. Other Israelites began to mobilize as well (Judges 6:35). Despite the miracle of what happened, Gideon struggled with trusting the Lord. So he laid out a fleece, and God again confirmed that He was with him.

Some Men Are Mighty; Others Are Reasonable[59]

Gideon's faithfulness in his personal life, family life, and church life set the stage for what one reads in Judges 7. In the English Standard Version Study Bible, the pericope title for chapter 7 is "Gideon's First Battle." This is true in

---

59 I learned this concept from my father, but I heard this particular phrase in a sermon from Pastor Douglas Wilson.

one sense, as it is Gideon's first time to face the Midianites in physical battle. But there's another sense where this is not true, because of what happened in chapter 6. In chapter 6, Gideon fought a battle of an arguably more intense and difficult nature. Chapter 6 was a war of Gideon and his servants against his family and church. Chapter 7 is a physical military battle with unbelieving oppressors (but as we will see, this battle does not involve much physical warring either).

The Midianites, Amalekites, and all the people of the East are said to be like locusts in abundance, and their camels without number, as the sand is on the seashore (Judges 7:12). In chapter 8, we're told that 120,000 were killed and 15,000 survived—so that means there are approximately 135,000. And they're staging to do what they've been doing, to plunder the land and destroy it.

But this time is different. Just south of them, across the valley, is Gideon's army of 32,000. They all know what the Midianites are planning to do, but they are going to push back. The momentum seems to be in the Israelites' favor, as God has shown favor to Gideon. They are gathered to go to war instead of hiding in holes and threshing wheat in their winepresses. They are gathered to resist the army that wants to destroy their inheritance. But this army is four times their size. From a numbers perspective, the odds don't look good.

What does God tell Gideon? He says, "The people with you are too many for me to give the Midianites into their hand, lest Israel boast over me, saying, 'My own hand has saved me'" (Judges 7:2). God says, "Too many." He says, "You guys might just think that you saved yourselves. Right now, the odds are against you, but I will make the odds impossible—and then give you victory so that you clearly know that it was Me who gave it to you."

God is so concerned about ensuring that His sovereignty is recognized and that all glory is given to Him that He gives Gideon orders to reduce the size of his army. He tells Gideon to tell the people, "Whoever is fearful and trembling, let him return home and hurry away from Mount Gilead" (Judges 7:3). The law gives several military exemptions to include those who are afraid (Deuteronomy 20) so that they won't cause others to fear. Over two-thirds of the army, 22,000 men, leave.

Gideon is left with 10,000 men, and God says, "Still too many." So He has Gideon do a bizarre test. Gideon takes them to a stream and watches how the men drink the water. The ones who kneel down to drink are sent home. The ones who lap it up like dogs and bring their hands to their mouths remain (Judges 7:6).

Why would God have Gideon do this type of screening with his army? Some commentators, like Josephus, think the "lappers" were actually afraid, and being compared to a dog is never a flattering description. However, others believe that those who brought the water to their mouths with their hands were more alert and ready for battle, unlike those who knelt. I believe it is the latter, because the trajectory of selection suggests getting rid of men who were unfit for battle, not retaining them. God wanted to make it clear that He was going to bring them victory; however, he was highly selective in the men he would use. The men he wanted to use were not afraid, and they were shrewd.

Gideon trims his army down to 300 men from 32,000. So it's now 300 versus 150,000. Every person in Gideon's army needs to kill 500 Midianites to secure a victory. Seems a little insane, and I imagine there were a few guys who were thinking the same thing.

What Gideon was doing looked foolish to carnal human reasoning. Why send these men away? They needed them all! Perhaps there were some who whispered among themselves that Gideon was being a bad leader by unnecessarily putting a heavier burden on the people of God. With everyone fighting, each man needed to kill only four Midianites. With only three hundred fighting, each man needed to kill 500. Gideon clearly lacked wisdom! Israel was finally at a point where they could be free from Midian's tyranny. Freedom was so close, and Gideon started sending men home! How many people would have told him that what he was doing was lunacy? How many people whispered among themselves, "What a prideful fool!" How many reasonable men came up to Gideon and said, "I don't think this is wise. This isn't prudent. This doesn't make any sense, and you're being reckless. You have a shot at victory here, and you're throwing it away. What a waste! You're an arrogant, prideful youth!"

If you've ever held any position of authority, you can imagine some of the things that those under Gideon's charge may have been saying. I was a platoon commander in the Marines for a few years, and there were times when I had to make decisions that were fairly reasonable, and I still remember overhearing some of my Marines grumbling about it. There were times when the platoon was unhappy with what I chose to do.

Now if this happens in normal everyday life with fairly reasonable decisions, how much more can be expected when God has you do something that appears to be suicide? A wise pastor once said that more Christians ought to pray this prayer: "Geronimo! Amen." Many Christians are drawn to the idea of doing incredible things for the kingdom, but it remains only an abstract romantic notion that they blog about or read in books. They don't actually live it. They don't actually need to pray, "Geronimo! Amen," because they aren't jumping off any cliffs. They aren't facing any giants. They aren't leading any 300-man armies against 150,000-man armies. But when you listen to God and obey, He will place you in situations where you will have to pray that prayer. Reasonable men don't need to pray this.

There will always be plenty of reasonable men to manage the status quo. But reasonable men don't take steps that go from ship to sea, as Peter did when he walked on water. Reasonable men don't go to war without armor, as David did. Reasonable men don't continue to preach a message that repeatedly gets them beaten, whipped, put in jail, and eventually killed, as the early Church martyrs did. Reasonable men don't preach that it's unlawful for Herod to have his brother's wife, as John the Baptist did. Reasonable men don't preach that divorce and remarriage is always adultery. No, this is not what reasonable men do. It is what faithful men do. God isn't looking for reasonable men. God is looking for obedient men. And it's that simple.

That's what Gideon is doing here: trusting God and doing. In obedience and martyrdom, God is glorified. In obedience and conquest, God is glorified. You cannot lose when you're trusting and obeying the Lord. But it takes courage, and often that courage looks like folly. If it didn't look like folly, it wouldn't be courage. We can always look back on history and surmise that we would be on the right side, but we have the luxury of knowing the outcome from the inception. This wasn't the case for Gideon, and it's not the case for us.

INTELLIGENCE REPORTS CONFIRM THAT THE BATTLE IS ALREADY WON

After Gideon has his three-hundred-man army, the Lord instructs him to conduct a reconnaissance mission inside the Midianite camp. So he and his servant Purah go down to the enemy camp and overhear a man telling his companion about a strange dream he had, that a loaf of bread tumbled into the Midianite camp, hit the tent, knocked it down, and flipped it over. His companion immediately offers an interpretation: "This is no other than the sword of Gideon the son of Joash, a man of Israel; God has given into his hand Midian and all the camp" (Judges 7:14). When I read this, I can't help but think that God has a sense of humor. One, it's a funny dream. Two, his companion interprets the dream immediately. Three, Gideon is listening.

Earlier in the story (chapter 6), Gideon is frequently struggling with fear and reassurance. And God continually reassures him through various signs and wonders. The angel of the Lord consumes Gideon's preparation of meat and unleavened cake with fire—a reassurance of Gideon's standing before the Lord. The Lord provides two miraculous signs with the fleece to assure Gideon that Israel will be delivered by his hand, and here we see God reassuring and comforting Gideon through the dreams of his enemies. How much more reassurance does this guy need?

But we are just as hesitant to trust the Lord. After God has told us a million times that the water is nice, we still only dip our toes in. Then we might slowly start to wade in from the shallow end. We rarely say, "Geronimo! Amen," and do a cannonball into the deep end of the pool. But that's what God wants us to do. And His patience in reassuring us is more than I can fathom, because a majority of people only stay in the shallow end and admire the great cannon-ballers of the past. They write books about them, post gushing praise of past cannonballers on social media, and then laugh at and mock and dismiss the cannonballers that they personally know. To speak out against divorce and remarriage in our divorce culture is to be a cannonballer. God has reassured us that the water is fine, so go ahead and make a splash!

After Gideon is reassured, he worships: "As soon as Gideon heard the telling of the dream and its interpretation, he worshiped. And he returned to the camp of Israel and said, 'Arise, for the Lord has given the host of Midian into your hand'" (Judges 7:15). Gideon has been given a preview in a dream of the victory Israel will have over their enemies. He immediately worships, and then he returns to his fellow Israelites to confidently say, "We're going to win; let's go to war." These dreams have given Gideon the confidence to go forward in the war.

God is pleased to tell His servants what He's planning to do: "For the Lord God does nothing without revealing his secret to his servants the prophets" (Amos 3:7).

In a greater, more eschatological sense, just as Gideon was given a preview of Israel's victory over Midian, all Christians have been given a preview of their victory over the world and over death. Jesus's resurrection is a preview of the future, and anyone who has been regenerated and baptized into Christ is a partaker of everything that is Christ's. Paul tells us that Jesus must reign until he has put all enemies under his feet and that the last enemy to be destroyed will be death (1 Corinthians 15). John's visions on Patmos, as recorded in the book of Revelation, are like a dream reassuring us of the victory of true Israel, the Church, over her enemies.

Scripture abounds with dreams, visions, and prophecies that reassure and comfort us about the coming victory. So we ought to follow Gideon's example in worshiping God for this and exhorting one another to confidently go into battle, because we have been given victory. Confronting the sin in your own life, your family's lives, your church, and your nation can be frightening, especially when it is the sin of unlawful, adulterous marriage. But proper interpretation of Scripture shows us that this sin is truly our enemy and that we will win the battle over it. Truth will ultimately be victorious. We can go forward, confidently worshiping the Lord and conquering His enemies, taking back the land that has been promised to us—which is the whole world.

THE WORD OF GOD / SOUNDING THE TRUMPET

The way in which Gideon takes back the land gives us insight into how Christians can take back the earth. Gideon gives his men trumpets, torches, and empty jars to put the torches in. Then he says, "Look at me, and do as I do" (Judges 7:17). He tells them that when he comes to the outside of the Midianite camp and blows the trumpet, then all his men are to blow their trumpets and shout, "A sword of the Lord and of Gideon." So they surround the enemy camp and do what Gideon instructed (Judges 7:12). They also smash the jars covering the torches. This sent the Midianite camp into a terrible frenzy, and they all turn on one another. So much so that 120,000 die—we find this number in the next chapter. God gave Israel the Midianites through the hand of Gideon, just as He promised and just as the dream indicated. The dream and the weapons of warfare typify Christ, the Holy Spirit, and speaking the word of God.

The Weapons of Warfare: Trumpets, Torches, and Words

In Scripture, trumpets are used in a variety of contexts and can mean different things. However, there are two instances I want to draw attention to. The first is that the sounding of a trumpet can signal going to war or launching an attack (Ezekiel 7:14, Jeremiah 51:27, and 1 Corinthians 14:8), which is what we expect to happen in the case of Gideon's army against the Midianites. The second is that the sounding of a trumpet signals the presence of God and the giving of His word at Sinai. A loud trumpet sounded when the law was given at Sinai, which caused all the people in the camp to tremble (Exodus 19:16), not unlike the sounding of the trumpets by Gideon's army, which caused all Midianites in the camp to tremble to such an extent that they began to butcher one another.

When Joshua destroyed Jericho, seven priests carried seven trumpets before the Ark of the Covenant, which contained the words of God, and blew the trumpets seven times each time they circled the city (which was seven times) (Joshua 6:4). Seven represents perfection—in this case, the perfection of God's word. The trumpets preceding the Ark of the Covenant represent the preaching of the perfect word of God and its power in warfare. All these examples typify the power of the word of God to conquer His enemies.

The men of Gideon's army carried their trumpets in one hand and torches in the other. The torch, consisting of fire and giving off light, represents Christ and the power of the Holy Spirit. Jesus declares that He is the light of the world (John 8). John the Baptist bore witness to the light in reference to Jesus (John 1). John the Baptist also says that Jesus will baptize with fire (Matthew 3:11-12). The Holy Spirit at Pentecost is accompanied by tongues of fire (Acts 2). So the torches of Gideon's army typify Christ and the Holy Spirit.

The earthen vessels, the pots, typify Christians or, more broadly, humanity. We are, after all, created from the earth, from clay, like pottery. The Children of Zion are described as earthen pitchers or jars (Lamentations 4). Paul describes humans as clay vessels (Romans 9). And I believe Paul makes an allusion to this very likeness in his epistle to the Corinthians (2 Corinthians 4:6-7). The torches hidden under the earthen vessels by Gideon's army symbolize the light of the knowledge of the glory of God in the hearts of Christians. Scripture teaches that we are like pottery. We are made from the earth and created for honorable or dishonorable use. And in the story of Gideon, the jars had to be shattered in order for the fire and light to shine uninhibited. Christians, too, must shatter themselves. We must break ourselves. We must say along with John the Baptist of Jesus, "He must increase and I must decrease." The self-denial of following Christ, of picking up your cross to follow him, is typified in the shattering of the jars. It is a picture of our own frailty and weakness, but also of God's power in us.

Last, the weapons of warfare include the spoken word. Everyone in Gideon's army cried, "The sword of the Lord and of Gideon" (Judges 7:20). Yet the swords of Gideon's army were never used. They simply spoke and caused the 120,000 Midianites to turn one another into pink mist. God spoke and created the world. Ezekiel spoke and gave life to bones. Jesus spoke and cast out demons. The apostles spoke and began to kill the pagan world. "Death and life are in the power of the tongue" (Proverbs 18:21). "How then will they call on him in whom they have not believed? And how are they to believe in him of whom they have never heard? And how are they to hear without someone preaching?" (Romans 10:14). Speaking, teaching, preaching—these are all weapons of warfare. God uses these means to kill the old man and to resurrect the new, to destroy spiritual principalities, to annihilate old worlds, and to create new ones.

All these things taken together—the sounding of a trumpet at the giving of the law and at the giving of the word of God, the sounding of trumpets by priests during the battle of Jericho and of Gideon's army, Christ and the Holy Spirit typified in the fire and light of the torches, and the use and power of words in warfare—point us to the proclamation and potency of the gospel of Christ in the war for the world.

And this is exactly what the Midianite dreamed. He dreamed of a barley cake, which is a loaf of bread, tumbling down into the camp and smashing the tent, turning it upside down. This typifies Christ, who is the bread of life (John 6:35). Jesus says, "I am the bread of life; whoever comes to me shall not hunger, and whoever believes in me shall never thirst." All those who come to Him are given sustenance, vitality, and satiation of their insatiable desires apart from Him. He gives life to our dying souls and worlds, and He will give life to our dead bodies.

Conversely, those who do not come and do not believe will be destroyed by the same bread. The seeming protection of a Midianite tent, of the securities of this world, will be decimated by Christ. Jesus is life giving to those who come to Him, and He is lethal to those who resist Him. Jesus is the bread of life, but He is also the bread of death, for He is a God who brings forgiveness and life to His people and judgment and death to His enemies. Paul says that those who eat and drink without discerning the body eat and drink judgment on themselves, which is why some in the Corinthian congregation were weak, sick, and dying (1 Corinthians 11). But, he says, "If we were more discerning with regard to ourselves, we would not come under such judgment" (1 Corinthians 11:31). Bread can give life, and it can take it away. Blessed be the name of the Lord.

What we've discussed so far is a magnificent typification of New Covenant violence. Gideon's violence toward himself, his family, and his church gave him victory when he enacted violence toward the unbelieving outside world. Christians will be successful in battles with Muslims, liberals, feminists, homosexuals, socialists, and so on only when we repent of our disobedience regarding divorce and remarriage in our own lives and the lives of our families, our friends, and our churches. We don't think we need to repent of those things, and so the Baals and Asherahs still stand tall in our churches. This is why we continue to lose as we go out to fight the Midianites, Amalekites, and people of the East. We are left scratching our heads and wondering why we lose, or we conjure up ridiculous reasons for why.

I cannot stress this enough. Our refusal to repent of adulterous marriages is the root reason we are losing. Repent of these things, and we will begin to convert the culture more effectively than we are doing now. We will preach the word, and the culture will tremble and turn on itself. We will have the heat of the Holy Spirit and sharpness of the Word killing the Adamic culture and resurrecting a Christian culture and magistrate. But we revert to this satanic desire to hold on to our little kingdoms at the expense of the kingdom. We would rather preserve our lives and let our brothers and sisters die than lose our lives so they may live.

Gideon told his men, "Look at me and do likewise" (Judges 7:17). His faith, at least at this point in his life, is worthy of emulation. He is, after all, listed in the hall of faith in Hebrews 11. Paul seems to echo these words in his first letter to the Corinthians: "Imitate me as I imitate Christ" (1 Corinthians 11:1).

Can you say this with conviction? Can you say, "Look at me, and do likewise"? Can you say, "Imitate me, as I imitate Christ"? We are to strive for this. We are to imitate Christ, who said things like, "I do as the Father has commanded me, so that the world may know that I love the Father" (John 14:31). When the world looks at you, do they know you love the Father? Has your earthiness been shattered enough to have the light of Christ and the Holy Spirit shine through? Are you engaged in worship and warfare through the proclamation of the Word to your family, to your sons and daughters, to your coworkers who know about Jesus but are only nominally Christian, or to your family member who is not a Christian? The word of God is powerful, and we are weak and unworthy vessels, yet we are to speak and proclaim. This is what we must do with everyone around us who is practicing and approving of adultery through divorce and remarriage. We must acknowledge that we are weak and frail vessels, but we need to proclaim the light of the gospel in a dark Church.

No Spark; No Fire

Repentance does not start with the world and then filter into the Church. Evangelical frenzy in the political and cultural sphere is misplaced because we have the diagnosis all wrong. We think the symptoms are the cause. If we could protest enough abortion clinics and get the Supreme Court to overturn the Obergefell ruling, then something might be cured. But this is like going to fight the Midianites before fighting the Baals and Asherahs in your family and church. This is not to say political involvement, artistic contributions, and economic activism are to be avoided. It is to say that the root problem is not bad economic or foreign policy or failure to make a law defining marriage; the core sickness is sin inside the Church, and the cure is repentance and obedience to Jesus Christ. Once the Church repents of her approval of divorce and remarriage, then we will begin to see tremendous victory in the social and political sphere.

A major reason for my writing this book is to connect the necessity of repenting of unlawful marriages in the Church with the victories it will subsequently garner. It is incredible that many Christians cannot see past the difficulties entailed with this form of repentance. Their minds get stuck on the horror of fake, unlawful families breaking up to follow Christ. It's this myopic objection that prevents them from understanding the nature of reformation. But a wise pastor once said something that pierces these objections more deeply than I believe he intended. In a sermon, he said, "Do you pray for reformation and revival in the Church? Well and good. You ought to. But if you pray for reformation and revival in the Church, you are praying for a mess. You are praying for a glorious spectacular mess. You are praying for God to do something that will fill you with consternation when you first begin to see it."[60] This is absolutely true. When reformation comes, the levels of divorce for unlawful marriages will skyrocket and will be a glorious mess that will fill you with consternation.

It will fill you with consternation because right now, Christians are allowed to disagree with divorce and remarriage only in an impotent, abstract, academic sense. They can only declare their disagreement and then simply

---

60 Douglas Wilson, Sermon: Samuel VI, *The Ark of Authority*.

agree to disagree with the adulterers in their church. But this isn't what God's law demands. As I said earlier, it wasn't enough for Gideon to simply disagree with his father's sinful worship and the sinful worship his father led the church in. He needed to make this belief public. It needed to have teeth. It needed to be acknowledged and enforced in the public arena.

This principle is played out in the political sphere between secularists and Christians all the time. Secularists believe that Christians can maintain their beliefs but they have to keep them private. A Christian's beliefs cannot manifest themselves in the public sphere, and they certainly cannot be given any enforceable priority. In other words, a Christian's beliefs are allowed only to be impotent and irrelevant. This is exactly how most of the Church leadership treats Christians who believe in traditional marriage. Christians are allowed to disagree with the practice of divorce and remarriage but are not allowed to extend those beliefs outward. They are not allowed to disassociate with adulterous Christians. They are not allowed to tell adulterous Christians that they must end their adulterous marriages or be excommunicated.

Secularists do the same thing. They say you are allowed to believe homosexuals are in sin (even though that's a hateful and bigoted thing to believe) but you are not allowed to legislate against homosexuality. Conservative Christian pastors say to the Christians who want to follow Christ in a divorce culture that they are allowed to believe that divorce and remarriage is adultery (even though that is a bigoted and hateful position) but they are not allowed to legislate against it—meaning they are not allowed to excommunicate these people from the Church if they refuse to repent. Christians are patted on the head and told "There, there" in the public realm because we do it to our own people in the ecclesiastical realm.

Unless we become like Gideon and tear down the entrenched sinful practices of our fellow Israelites, despite our friends' and families' disapproval, we will never drive the enemies out. But this will be costly, just as it cost Joash his bulls, just as it cost the Gerasenes their pigs. The cleansing of the demoniac did not happen without the loss of precious things. Christ eradicated the tyranny. He brought purity and peace, but then the recipients of that peace became angry with Him. The Benefactor angers the beneficiaries.

We must be willing to do the same. We must be willing to obey Jesus no matter the cost. We must be willing to repent personally for our sins. We must be willing to confront the sins of our families, to do what Gideon did and Ham did not. And we must be willing to do this trusting that God will be with us no matter the outcome. These things were necessary to defeat Midian. These things are necessary preliminaries to cultural and political victory. These things are the sparks to reformation fire.

CHAPTER 7

GRACE IS A SLAUGHTERHOUSE

―――

JEHU, LIKE GIDEON, IS ANOTHER great example of the kind of men we need in a Church ruled by manipulative Jezebels and weak-willed Ahabs. In 2 Kings 9 (and 10), we find a record of God's grace toward Israel in His sending of Jehu, a warrior-king, to relieve them of their wicked rulers and to restore proper worship. It is a story that reads like a Quentin Tarantino script, which is to say it is an exceptionally violent passage. It is a bloodbath. Didn't the Lord know that families would be reading this? God is gracious, but grace is violent. With blood comes cleansing. There may be forgiveness, but someone still has to die. God forgives our sins, but only because we are put to death in Christ's death. "It is the blood, given in exchange for a life, that makes purification possible" (Leviticus 17:11). The judgment on Ahab's house was a means of grace to Israel's house.

ISRAEL'S CRESCENDO OF EVIL

Under King David, all Israel is united. The unity continues under Solomon, and then after Solomon, his son Rehoboam reigns as king in Judah in the south, and Jeroboam breaks off with Israel in the north. Then there is a succession of four wicked kings in Israel, with Omri being the fifth, who does "more evil than all who were before him" (1 Kings 16:25). This is Ahab's father. Ahab, once he becomes king, does "more evil than all who were before him" (1 Kings 16:30). Evil increases as the succession of kings continues. Ahab's reign is the sinful climax. Then God unleashes Jehu in a killing spree, which annihilates everyone associated with Ahab. What did Ahab do (or omit to do) to bring about this judgment?

Scripture tells us that Ahab considered it a light thing to walk in the sins of Jeroboam (1 Kings 16:31), which means to facilitate golden-calf worship—idolatry. The similarities between Aaron and Jeroboam are striking. They both set up golden calves for the Israelites to worship. Jeroboam says, "This is the god who brought you out of Egypt," just as the people under Aaron had said (Exodus 32:4; 1 Kings 12:28). Both Aaron and Jeroboam made decisions about how to worship, based on the will of the people rather than on the will of God (Exodus 32:1–2; 1 Kings 12:26–28). Jeroboam's reasoning was entirely self-serving too. He wanted to allow the people to worship God without having to travel to Jerusalem to do so, because if they did, he risked the possibility of their hearts turning away from Jeroboam and to the king of Judah instead. Then they would kill Jeroboam. So he set up a golden calf in Bethel and in Dan.[61] Aaron did a similar thing after the people had already turned on Moses. These sins were committed out of self-preservation. They both buckled to the will of the people. They did not want to be firm with the people but instead gave them what they wanted. In both cases, these men would have lost their positions of authority, or more likely, they would have lost their lives.

This is precisely the sin that pastors commit when they buckle to the pressures of the people regarding divorce and remarriage. The people want to worship God on their own terms, not on God's terms. They get tired of waiting for their estranged spouses to repent. They get frustrated with always being the bridesmaid but never the bride. They get engaged to nice Christian men who also happen to be divorced. Divorced Christian women talk about how their spouses were the worst possible sinners ever, even worse than Hitler.

---

61 The reference to idols set up in Bethel and Dan could possibly be a literary device indicating that idol worship was set up in all Israel, not exclusively in Bethel and Dan. Bethel is in the extreme south, while Dan is in the extreme north. When it says that these idols were set up in Bethel and Dan, it's possible that it's like saying McDonald's can be found on the East Coast and the West Coast of the United States, which is to say that McDonald's can be found in every state.

No, they *were* Hitler. "My situation was bad, right?" they say. "I'm a victim. Feel sorry for me. God feels sorry for me, and He allows me to exercise unforgiveness and covenant breaking as a result." Every situation is always a horror story. Every story is always the worst possible scenario. Every story always evokes pity. Every story always places God's approval on the remarriage and tells how godly and wonderful the new-and-improved spouse is.

There is no end to the horrific situations we can imagine or recall from our own experiences. But the point is that the people love their remarriages—they take on this messianic status in their ability to redeem the situation. So you, as their churchmate or pastor, can't take that away from them, because then the people will turn on you or go to a different church. Therefore, pastors begin to craft an idol in the shape of a golden theology that allows their people to worship God through adulterous marriages. Give me your tithes, and I will fashion them into an idol you can pretend to worship the Triune God with. This permits them to put down the cross of their legitimate marriages and finally be "happy" in marriages God says are adultery.

The leaders of God's people have a history of caving in to the demands of the people out of self-preservation. The leaders give the people what they want. They think they are being clever by saying that the people can worship God in this way. Perhaps the leaders really believe they are being faithful. Perhaps Aaron truly believed he was being faithful. Either way, he wasn't, and neither are the pastors who permit this idolatry. They are walking in the sins of Jeroboam.

Ahab walked in the sins of Jeroboam and considered it a trivial thing. This is the sin that all the kings following Jeroboam were guilty of, but Ahab considered it trivial—just like our ministers today consider divorce and remarriage to be a trivial thing. They give lip service to the lamentable state of affairs of marriage, but they defend tooth and nail the right of their parishioners to divorce and remarry. They will defend with more tenacity the right of a person to stay in an adulterous remarriage than they will defend the command for a person to stay in a lawful marriage. It's insanity. The insanity of Ahab.

In addition to the insanity of facilitating God's people to sin the way they wanted, Ahab took a wife, Jezebel, the daughter of Ethbaal, king of the

Sidonians. Ethbaal simply means "with Baal" or "toward Baal." Ethbaal is not only a king but likely a priest as well.[62] So Jezebel is the daughter of a priest-king of a false religion, and we are told that Ahab served Baal and worshiped him after he married Jezebel (1 Kings 16). "But there was no one like Ahab who sold himself to do wickedness in the sight of the Lord, because Jezebel his wife stirred him up" (1 Kings 21:25).

This also is a major problem with Christian men in the Church. They are ruled by their wives. It is ubiquitous in popular culture, and it is the ugly underbelly of the Church. Men submit to their wives and worship God wrongly in order to preserve their marriages. They worship self-preservation and their wives more than they worship God. They are unwilling to lose their wives for the sake of following Christ. If they were to follow Christ, then their wives wouldn't be able to have the bourgeois social life that comes with associating with adulterers—those who are divorced and remarried. It would totally destroy the little kingdoms that they envision having. The Jezebel women in our churches will not let their husbands ruin that, and so they manipulate them in order to get what they want. They gaslight. They withhold sex. They pester. "And it came to pass, when she pestered him daily with her words and pressed him, so that his soul was vexed to death" (Judges 16:16). They whine. They pout. They turn cold. They threaten. And men just bow down to their demands, like negotiating with terrorists.

Christian men need to adopt America's foreign policy when it comes to their terrorist wives. America doesn't negotiate with terrorists, and neither should you. But since they do negotiate and they submit to Eve's will, death comes in. They throw the protection of Christ out of their lives, and the consequences are death and sickness. All this is really the sin of Adam repeated again, which we will get into later.

Of course, not all wives are this way. Many are godly helpers to their husbands, and I am profoundly grateful for them. I am speaking anecdotally here of manipulative Christian women, which could be totally different from your

---

62 See Josephus's citation of the Phoenician author Menander of Ephesus in *Against Apion* i.18.

experience, but this is what I have witnessed, and it is also blatantly pervasive in popular culture, which cannot be disputed.

Jeroboam at least pretended to worship Jehovah God. Ahab served an entirely different God—Baal. We see this happening in our culture too. Our leaders are forsaking the worship of the God of Abraham, Isaac, and Jacob for other gods entirely—the god of self, the god of Islam, the god of Eastern mysticism, the god of science, and so on. Ahab built a temple of Baal in Samaria and built Asherah poles. Some translations say Asherah, and some say "a wooden image." These terms are interchangeable. Ahab is in direct violation of Deuteronomy 16:21, which says, "You shall not plant for yourself any tree, as a wooden image, near the altar which you build for yourself to the Lord your God." How could a ruler of Israel be in direct violation of the word of God?

We see this happening in our culture too. In the Church, we have gone directly against the word of God by saying a woman is not bound to her husband as long as she lives—a direct violation of Jesus's and Paul's words. This rebellion has bred symptomatic rebellions that have subsequently been institutionalized as well, such as abortion and homosexuality. But the institutionalized sin of divorce and remarriage begat these latter institutionalized sins. The sins just accumulate, and we begin to see the sin become more clearly antithetical to God's words, just as the sins of Israel, and Ahab in particular, progressively became more opposed to God's word.

How else did Ahab sin? He practiced filicide—the same type of sin as abortion. He rebuilt Jericho by sacrificing his children. He laid his first-born son at its foundation, and with his youngest son, he set up the gates (1 Kings 16:34). This was in violation or fulfillment of what Joshua had pronounced after their victory over Jericho: "Cursed before the LORD be the man who rises up and rebuilds this city, Jericho. At the cost of his first-born shall he lay its foundation, and at the cost of his youngest son shall he set up its gates" (Joshua 6:26). This is exactly what Ahab did. The word of God said anyone who did this would be cursed, and Ahab did it anyway. It is high-handed rebellion, but somehow Ahab was convinced that it was a good idea.

This, again, is exactly what the Church leadership is doing. They build cities by sacrificing their children. It's precisely what happened to the church in Thyatira that tolerated the woman Jezebel. They were seduced by Jezebel, and their children began to die as a result. The leadership in the Church is ruled by this spirit of Jezebel, and their children are dying. The children of people in the Church are either physically dying or spiritually dying. Additionally, the Church is not begetting children in an evangelistic sense—people aren't being converted or being born again. The Church, which is supposed to be our mother, is supposed to nourish her children, but when the Church is ruled by Jezebel, she aborts her children.

This is then played out in culture when women desire to live a certain kind of life and need to murder their children in order to do so. And men, their husbands or partners, and abortion doctors facilitate them in this by killing their children either directly or indirectly by pressuring them into it. The womb is supposed to be the safest place for a child, but it's the most dangerous place for a child—just as the Church is right now. Instead of the Church being the mother of us all, as Paul describes her, she has instead become the antimother of us all. Just as women sacrifice their children so they can go to college and make money, the antimother Church sacrifices her children to build the Jerichos of a comfortable life—sipping coffee and having people over for dinner. The Church is an ecclesiastical Planned Parenthood. She is an abortion mill run by Jezebel and Ahab.

Jezebel and Ahab are murderers not only of their children but also of people who have things they want. Jezebel kills Naboth so that they can take his vineyard. She murders to get what she wants. This wife of Ahab is a real sweetheart. She does what the Jezebel spirit in our churches does. We want to be part of a beautiful vineyard in the kingdom. We want a vibrant social life. We want to eat the fruits of vineyards that are off-limits to us. We want another man's wife. We want another woman's husband. We are unsatisfied with our own vineyard. So we murder to get what we want.

The pinnacle of wickedness under Ahab's reign occurs when Jezebel massacres the prophets of the Lord (1 Kings 18:4). She even continues this after a clear demonstration of Baal's inferiority to the true God of Israel at Mount

Carmel (1 Kings 18). Jezebel simply does not care. She wants to worship a certain way despite all the evidence to the contrary. So Jezebel continues her attempts to kill all the prophets of Jehovah God and to kill Elijah particularly after the showdown at Mount Carmel. It is this kind of recognition of God and who He is and what is undeniably true, coupled with an obstinate rejection of it and refusal to bend the knee to Him, that causes Ahab's house to be cut off (2 Kings 9:7).

I have seen women (and some men) terrified at the prospect of Christ's words being truly implemented in worship. They would lose their lives—the lives they have envisioned for themselves, the kind of lives that keeps Christ and His followers at manageable and tolerable levels. So when that is threatened by clear demonstrations of God's power and word, they will go to any measure to destroy the prophets of God. Just as John the Baptist was Elijah, Herodias was Jezebel. Herodias didn't like that John the Baptist had been telling her that her marriage was unlawful, as it was both the product of divorce and remarriage and a violation of consanguinity. So she had his head cut off. Jezebels will do whatever they must in order to maintain the status quo.

It can be terrifying to have that kind of violent witchcraft directed toward you, and those of you who have chosen to follow Christ already know what I'm talking about. But for those of you who will decide to stand up against Ahab and Jezebel, you will be attacked. She will try to assassinate you by bearing false witness against you. She will breathe out lies as long as it removes you and justifies her (1 Kings 21:8–10). Those who love the kingdom more than the king will say what Jezebel said when they find out that you are preaching the word of God against the prophets of Baal—the defenders of divorce and remarriage.

Your spiritual execution of the false prophets will be returned by them. The spirits of these Jezebels punch back. They will say, "So let the gods do to me, and more also, if I do not make your life as the life of one of them by tomorrow about this time" (1 Kings 19:2). You might even become afraid, just as Elijah was. But God encouraged Elijah by telling him what he would do to Jezebel and Ahab with Jehu and that there were others in Israel who had not bent the knee to Baal (1 Kings 19:17–18). Brothers and sisters in the Lord, I want to remind you that there are many others who have not bent the knee to the Baal of adulterous marriage, and there are also Jehus among us who are being unleashed as you read this.

Jehu is released only after Ahab dies. This is because Ahab repents toward the end of his life, and God spares him and his house until he passes away. God is merciful, but He is still just. As soon as Ahab dies, God unleashed Jehu on Ahab's house, as recorded in 2 Kings 9.

THE KINGDOM OF HEAVEN SUFFERS VIOLENCE, AND VIOLENT MEN TAKE IT BY FORCE

At this time, around 752 BC, Israel is at war with the Syrians. Jehu is a captain of the Israelite army. His name roughly translates to "Jehovah is He," which ought to be kept in mind, as Jehu is clearly a type of Christ. The Lord already revealed to Elijah what Jehu would do and that he would anoint him: "You shall anoint Jehu the son of Nimshi as king over Israel. And Elisha the son of Shaphat of Abel Meholah you shall anoint as prophet in your place. It shall be that whoever escapes the sword of Hazael, Jehu will kill; and whoever escapes the sword of Jehu, Elisha will kill" (1 Kings 19:15–18). The anointing of Jehu begins 2 Kings 9. Elisha sends a son of a prophet in his place. This prophet's son acts as a representative of Elisha and, ultimately, Elijah.

This representative is sent to anoint Jehu. The whole scene foreshadows the interactions between John the Baptist and Jesus. The Elijah figure anoints the messianic figure. If you are willing to accept it, Elijah inaugurates Jehu's ministry, just as John the Baptist inaugurates the ministry of Jesus with His baptism. Jesus says of John the Baptist, "If you are willing to accept it, he is Elijah" (Matthew 11:13). Elijah's mantle has been given to Elisha who, in turn, has given it to this prophet's son. It is worth noting the descending obscurity from Elijah to a nameless son of a prophet because of John's words: "He must increase, but I must decrease" (John 3:30).

Jehu's servants refer to Elijah as a "madman" (2 Kings 9:11). Jehu says of the nameless son of a prophet, "You know the man and his babble." This seems to indicate that this man had a reputation for being a little off. If you think of John the Baptist, with his camel's hair and bug-eating diet, he likely had a similar reputation.

The madman finds Jehu, an officer in the Israeli Defense Force, and promotes him to the Israeli prime minister. He anoints him with oil. Anointing with oil is associated with a myriad of things, among them the identification and commissioning of kings. Samuel anoints Saul and David by pouring a flask of oil on their heads. The word Messiah comes from the Hebrew word for "anointed." The word Christ comes from the Greek word for "anointed." So the anointing of Jehu has the meaning of his both becoming Israel's king immediately and typologically signifying the ultimate king of Israel—Christ. Jehu is a shadow of the Anointed One.

The instructions Elisha gives to the prophet's son reveal more about this messianic shadow. Elisha tells him to anoint Jehu and run away. He says that once he anoints him, he is to open the door and flee and not delay (2 Kings 9:3). This indicates that Jehu's ascension as king was going to be a dangerous event. Anointing Jehu was like lighting the fuse to a bomb. Easton's *Bible Dictionary* describes Jehu like this: "He was one of those decisive, terrible, and ambitious, yet prudent, calculating, and passionless men whom God from time to time raises up to change the fate of empires and execute his judgments on the earth."[63]

I'm reminded of a scene from *The Lion, the Witch and the Wardrobe*. Lucy is talking with Mr. and Mrs. Beaver about Aslan, and Lucy asks whether he's safe. Mr. Beaver says, "Safe? Don't you hear what Mrs. Beaver tells you? Who said anything about safe? Course he isn't safe. But he's good. He's the King, I tell you."[64] This is what Jehu is like. This is what Jesus is like. He is a warrior-king who is not tame. He is not safe. He is not toothless. But he is good.

As soon as Jehu is publicly declared king, everyone presents their garments and put them under him on the top of the steps, and they blow trumpets, saying, "Jehu is king!" (2 Kings 9:12–13). Jehu is king, and they celebrate this

---

63 Easton, M. G. (1893). In *Easton's Bible dictionary*. New York: Harper & Brothers.
64 C. S. Lewis, *The Chronicles of Narnia: The Lion, The Witch, and the Wardrobe* (New York: Harper Collins Publishers, 1950), 80.

coronation in a show of solidarity by spreading their cloaks on the ground, an act of homage to royalty. This is also exactly what the people do when Jesus comes riding into Jerusalem on a donkey—the triumphal entry. They spread their cloaks on the ground and put palm branches before him in an act of homage recognizing him as their king. This event appears in all four gospels. And all the people shout, "Blessed is the King who comes in the name of the Lord!" (Mark 19:38). The Christological typology is striking.

The accounts of the triumphal entry in the synoptic gospels are all followed by various forms of Jesus pronouncing judgment on Israel/Jerusalem symbolically by His cursing the fig tree (in Matthew 21:1–22 and Mark 11:1–24), which is more harsh, or by His weeping over the city, which is more compassionate (Luke 19:28–48, a fascinating contrast showing the full spectrum of Jesus's humanity), and pronouncing His judgment in more explicit terms. In all three synoptics, the curse on the fig tree is done in tandem with the cleansing of the temple, Jesus's most zealous and Jehu-like episode. Jehu's judgment on unfaithful Israel typifies Jesus's judgment on unfaithful Israel, the destruction of Jerusalem in AD 70.

Aye, Aye, Sir!

Jehu is authorized by God to destroy the Ahab regime. Being a good Christian man, Jehu obeys quickly, zealously, and with wisdom. His first act of obedience as king is to plan the assassination of the king of Israel, Joram, whom he has replaced (2 Kings 9:14). Jehu is shrewd, just as Jesus tells Christians to be (Matthew 10:16). Jehu puts the city he's in, Ramoth Gilead, on lockdown to ensure that no one notifies Joram that he is coming to put him six feet under. The element of surprise is always key in two areas of life: telling jokes and assassinating heads of state. Jehu knew this. He was smart.

Jehu knew how to use the sword, but he also knew how to use his wits. The followers of Christ in our degenerate divorce culture will find themselves at odds with the unbelieving world, as Jehu was with Syria, and at odds with the Church, as Jehu was with Israel. So it is important that you enter into this battle strategically, as Jehu did.

Reformations, like wars, are messy. When you decide to obey Christ instead of your heretical pastor, you will be branded a traitor. You will be despised. You will be labeled unclean, angry, sinful, bitter, and so forth. Jehu received his training in an army led by the house of Ahab. In a sense, it was Jezebel's army. He was fighting as an officer in their army, protecting the house of Ahab from foreign invaders. And then he got the word from the Lord to systematically destroy the house of Ahab, and he obeyed.

How could Jehu go against the elders of his church? How could he go after the leaders of Israel? Because Jehu was a man of authority. Jehu's recognition of God's authority provided him with the organizing principle by which he could prioritize competing authorities. We must submit to and honor the elders in our churches, but when the authority of the men in your church collides with the authority of God, you must follow God instead. This is the principle by which we can successfully navigate the chaos of reformation.

Jehu was anointed king, but he knew that he was not the King of Kings. As an Israeli Defense Force special-forces captain, Jehu understood what it was to submit to authority and to exercise authority. Jesus marveled at another military officer who understood authority (Matthew 8:5–13). The Roman Centurion told Jesus, "Lord, I am not worthy to have you come under my roof, but only say the word, and my servant will be healed. For I too am a man under authority, with soldiers under me. And I say to one, 'Go,' and he goes, and to another, 'Come,' and he comes, and to my servant, 'Do this,' and he does it." The Lord told Jehu to do this, and he did it.

Believing that authority matters is closely tied with faith. It allows the person who hears the word of God to believe that the word of God cannot be broken and must be obeyed. Faith believes that the word of God is surer than the laws of physics and more certain than statistical probabilities. Abraham understood the authority of God's word to him regarding his posterity, and so he knew that if he were to sacrifice Isaac, God could bypass the laws of nature and bring Isaac back from the dead (Hebrews 11:19). Gideon knew that God had already promised him victory, so he believed that his army of 300 men would beat the Midianite army of 150,000 men. Jehu knew that God had anointed him king and ordered him to lead a coup against the house of Ahab, so he did, and he did so successfully. God's word is the only authority that matters. All other lesser authorities, whether they are laws of physics, probabilities, elders in your church, or heads of state, must bend the knee to God's word.

This is almost entirely lost on defenders of adulterous marriage. They always limit the authority of God. They reveal their unbelief. God says that divorce and remarriage is adultery and that we must repent of adultery. God says repentance means forsaking sin. This means that those who are in adulterous marriages need to separate. But the objections that people raise are always fueled by the unbelieving presuppositions. Their starting point is not the authority of God. It is looking at the outcomes of repentance and seeing it as being more damaging to everyone involved than if they stayed together. "But what about the kids?" What about the kids? If God says this is sin, then separate. Staying together will be worse for the kids than separating. By staying together, you teach your kids that you don't really trust God and that you don't want to obey Him. You also bring a curse on them and/or their children.

I've seen this happen, and I have no doubt that you can observe it happening in your own church. People who are divorced and remarried or associate with those who are have kids or grandkids who are unbelievers, divorced and remarried themselves, homosexuals, and/or pedophiles. This is tragic. This is the sin of Ham, which we discussed above.

To argue by any other authority than the word of God is like Sarah arguing with Abraham this way: "But you can't kill Isaac! That's not loving. In fact, Abraham, it would be sinful for you to sacrifice Isaac, because this is the son that God promised to us. Don't you want to glorify God by honoring this child that God miraculously gave to us? You are going against God's will by sacrificing him, Abraham! Repent of your cultish ideas!" This is the kind of sinful reasoning that I hear from people who want to defend the acceptability of adulterous lifestyles among their friends, family, and ultimately themselves. They reject God's authority for their own. They are clever, but they are evil arguments. Make no mistake about it. These arguments are evil because they reject God's authority as being foundational. They don't believe that God can preserve the children from the difficulties attendant in repenting via separation from an adulterous covenant. If they were talking to Abraham, they wouldn't believe that God could raise Isaac from the dead either. These people do not trust God. They do not have the kind of faith talked about in Hebrews 11.

After the Lord told Abraham to sacrifice his only son, whom he loved, he woke up early the next morning and immediately left to do it. He immediately did what he was supposed to do. He did not tarry. He did not wait. He did not dither. He was swift in his obedience. Jehu was the same way. He immediately obeyed God. This is the kind of obedience God is looking for. He wants men who will do cannonballs into the deep end when told to. Men who will jump out of planes without a parachute, men who are willing to be thrown into furnaces and into lions' dens, men who want to fight unbaptized Philistine giants, and men who go to the Place of the Skull to be slaughtered.

PEACE, PEACE, WHEN THERE IS NO PEACE

We live in a time when conservative pastors proclaim peace to adulterers when there is no peace—these people are going to hell if they don't repent by separating. The conservative Church has become the house of Ahab and doesn't realize it. They see only that we are at war with Syria, as the house of Ahab was in 2 Kings 9. They see only that we are at war with an unbelieving culture and liberal Christians. They believe they are innocent. They proclaim peace in their churches, which are gas chambers, whorehouses, and abortion mills. Everyone Jehu confronted asked whether he would be reasonable and proclaim peace to them as they had been doing, but Jehu knew the peace they wanted involved compromise with sin. So Jehu didn't bring peace. He brought war.

Jehu rides to Jezreel to assassinate Joram, and as he's riding, a watchman sees Jehu and his cohort. The watchman of the city sends messengers to him, asking, "Is it peace?" (2 Kings 9:18–20). This is done twice, and both times Jehu responds by saying, "What have you to do with peace? Turn around and follow me." It looks as though this is what both messengers do, because they don't return.

When Joram goes out to meet Jehu, he asks the same: "Is it peace?" Jehu responds more bluntly here: "What peace, as long as the harlotries of your mother Jezebel and her witchcraft are so many?" (2 Kings 9:22). Jehu basically asks, "How can there be peace when your slutty witch mother is around and approving of others who practice these things?" The paramount concern for everyone on the wrong side here is peace. The paramount concern of Jehu is righteousness. And Jehu calls them out on it. How can there be peace when we have compromised with sin?

How can there be peace when you have given your sons and daughters away to divorced men and women? Does this not approve of a practice that, if not repented, will deprive them of inheriting the kingdom? How can there be peace when your conservative daughters learn how to manipulate men, like their mother Jezebel? How can there be peace when your sons and daughters go off to college and give themselves to all kinds of debauchery? How can there be peace when the sins of covenant breaking that you condone cause your infants to die? Jehu is saying compromise with sin is incompatible with notions of peace.

Jehu understands how deadly compromise with sin is and that the nature of sin is imperialistic. This means that if you allow it in, there won't be peace but will be only more and more sin, which means more and more death. Look at our culture of death now. The sins we have compromised with have taken over your family, church, culture, and politics.

Sin is not content with compromise. The first place compromise occurs is in the heart of the individual. You think that it's not a big deal to give in a little here and a little there. But those small compromises then become larger compromises, and it becomes easier to give more and more territory to sin. That's what the enemy wants. He wants you to slowly surrender to more and more sin. Sin is constantly warring against your flesh, and it's not content until it has all of you, all your family, all your church, and all your country.

So we are left with this: there is no peace with sin until it destroys you or until you destroy it. Teddy Roosevelt is attributed with saying, "If I must choose between righteousness and peace, I choose righteousness." This is exactly what every Christian must do to follow Christ in this degenerate divorce culture. They must consider their safety, accolades, reputations, and security to be a pile of garbage compared to the righteousness of obedience and the warfare that comes with it. The Christian life is marked with conflict. Welcome to the war.

Ezekiel warns against false prophets who deny the war: "They have misled my people, saying, 'Peace,' when there is no peace" (Ezekiel 13:10). In speaking of Israel's rebellion, Jeremiah says, "They have healed the brokenness of My people superficially, Saying, 'Peace, peace,' But there is no peace" (Jeremiah 6:14). Don't think that compromise with sin will gain you anything but death. The kind of peace offered in that compromise is Munich Agreement peace. Neville Chamberlain, the prime minister of England, returned from Germany after making a compromise with Hitler. On the eve of one of the deadliest wars in human history, Chamberlain uttered the famous words, "I have attained peace in our time." A few years later, England was in flames.

Matthew Henry describes it this way: "What peace can come to that house in which there is so much wickedness unrepented of? Note, the way of sin can never be the way of peace, Isa. 57:21. What peace can sinners have with God, what peace with their own consciences, what good, what comfort, can they expect in life, in death, or after death, who go on still in their trespasses? No peace so long as sin is persisted in; but, as soon as it is repented of and forsaken, there is peace"[65]

This is what needs to happen in the Church. The sin of divorce and remarriage needs to be repented of and forsaken. Pastors need to repent of their facilitation of this sexual immorality and then rise up like Phinehas and put to death (through excommunication) anyone who continues to commit sexual immorality. Once this happens, as with Phinehas, the plague will stop, and there will be true peace.

WITCH-HUNTING SEASON IS OPEN

The judgment on the house of Ahab continues as Jehu kills Joram, the king of Israel, Ahab's son. He also kills Ahaziah, the king of Judah, Ahab's

---

65 Matthew Henry's Commentary on 2 Kings 9 available at biblegateway.com.

grandson. We see here again that the sins of Ahab and Jezebel create a Planned Parenthood facility right in the middle of the Church. Joram is killed because of Jezebel's murder of Naboth (2 Kings 9:25–26). Jehu is sent as an angel of death on the children of Ahab's house. The children of the sinful parents who refused to put the blood of the Lamb on their doorposts by their unwillingness to repent of their own sin and refusal to confront the sin of others are being aborted, just like conservative Christians who refuse to confront their own sin and the sin of those who are in their families and churches. The Lord God avenges the blood of His servants. When the leadership in the Church facilitates the deaths of His people through divorce and remarriage, God visits His vengeance on them and all who approve of their murder.

Jezebel hears what happened and puts on makeup, does her hair, and looks out the window for Jehu to arrive (2 Kings 9:30). There are a couple of things going on here. When the Bible uses this language of putting on makeup and doing hair, it's often in reference to preparation for sexual intimacy (see Jeremiah 4:30 and Ezekiel 23:40). So we get a glimpse into the type of woman Jezebel is. We already know she has control issues. She does whatever it takes to get her way, including murder. This verse, along with the previous reference to her harlotry, seems to indicate that she employs her sexuality to get her way. Jezebel does anything to stay in control. Notice she is surrounded by eunuchs, men she can control. She also places herself in a balcony window, looking down on Jehu, so as to be in the superior position. She likes to be in control. But she can't control Jehu. Jehu is no eunuch.

This Jezebel behavior comes to surface in some Christians when you begin to threaten their perverted worship. If you say that divorce and remarriage is adultery and that those who are in adulterous marriages need to separate, they will do everything in their power to control you and shut you up, to get you to bend the knee to their false idolatrous worship. You must realize that when this happens, it is not necessarily the person that is coming against you but the spirit of Jezebel. It is similar to what happens when Peter tries to persuade Jesus that He does not need to suffer and die. Jesus rebukes Satan. Women and men in the Church are, unfortunately, animated by this spirit of Jezebel, which wants to control, manipulate, and kill the prophets.

The end of the improper Baal worship in Israel is symbolized here. When we are told that Jezebel was looking through the window, it's evocative of a "woman in the window" motif found on carved ivory plaques in various ancient Near Eastern sites.[66] These plaques seem to suggest a representation of one of the wives of Baal, the goddess Astarte. If this is the case, this scene depicts Jezebel as the incarnation of the false religion Jezebel brought to Israel and her overthrow as congruous with the overthrow of Baal worship.

When Jehu arrives, Jezebel asks the same question everyone else on the wrong side of this war has been asking: "Is it peace?" But she also adds, "Zimri murderer of your master." She's taunting him. Zimri was another military officer in Israel's history who conspired against and successfully killed his king (1 Kings 16:9). But Zimri's reign as king lasted only a week. She's essentially saying two things: that he's a traitor, a Benedict Arnold who murders those he is supposed to protect, and that his reign as king will not last long.

This kind of thing is also typical of Jezebels in the Church. They will take whatever you're doing and turn it into a bad thing. They turn you into the bad guy. They are defending the sin in the Church, but they will say that you are a traitor. They will say that you are murdering those you are supposed to protect, when it is they who are facilitating the murder of their brothers and sisters in Christ. The Jezebel spirit, like Jezebel herself, is strong and defiant. Jezebel is provoking and resisting the prophets of God right up until her death.

As Jezebel is taunting Jehu, Jehu says, "Who's on my side?" Two or three eunuchs look out, and Jehu says, "Throw her down." So they throw her down, blood splatters all over, and Jehu smashes her some more with his horse to make sure she's dead. Then he goes inside and has dinner, while the dogs outside have Jezebel for dinner (2 Kings 9:30–37).

Many commentators have found fault with how Jehu so zealously destroyed the house of Ahab. This comes from a verse in Hosea that reads, "I will avenge the bloodshed of Jezreel on the house of Jehu, and bring an end to the kingdom of the house of Israel" (Hosea 1:4). But following the slaughter

---

66 Janet Howe Gaines, "Jezebel," *Bible Review* (2000). http://www.biblicalarchaeology.org/daily/people-cultures-in-the-bible/people-in-the-bible/how-bad-was-jezebel/#note06r.

of the house of Ahab, God highly commends Jehu by saying, "Because you have done well in doing what is right in My sight, and have done to the house of Ahab all that was in My heart, your sons shall sit on the throne of Israel to the fourth generation" (1 Kings 10:30). So I do not believe the Lord found fault with how Jehu destroyed the house of Ahab. God was pleased with this.

What He wasn't pleased with was that Jehu didn't go far enough. Jehu wasn't zealous enough. He didn't tear down all the idols. We are told this: "However Jehu did not turn away from the sins of Jeroboam the son of Nebat, who had made Israel sin, that is, from the golden calves that were at Bethel and Dan…but Jehu took no heed to walk in the law of the Lord God of Israel with all his heart; for he did not depart from the sins of Jeroboam, who had made Israel sin" (2 Kings 10:29, 10:31). Under Jehu's son, Jehoahaz, Israel is given over to Syria and slaughtered (2 Kings 13:1–7). I believe this is what Hosea is referring to when he mentions judgment for the blood of Jezreel: judgment not for Jehu doing what he had been commanded to do and what God said was "right in My sight" but for the blood spilled in Israel by the Syrians because of the continuation of the idol-worship facilitation known as the sins of Jeroboam.

Weak Men and Manipulative Women

This annihilation by Jehu took place because of the sins of Ahab and Jezebel, especially for the killing of God's servants and prophets (2 Kings 9:7). Ahab was a weak man who wanted to preserve himself, preserve his marriage, and preserve his kingdom at the expense of obedience to God. He was the result of a long line of men who refused to obey the Lord and endure the attendant conflict. He preserved his job as king by giving the people the idolatrous calf worship they wanted. He preserved his marriage by giving his wife the Baal worship she wanted, which, in turn, caused Israel to worship Baal with him. He obeyed the voice of everyone except God.

Imagine what would have happened if Ahab had obeyed God's voice instead of Jezebel's and the people's. Jezebel would have withheld sex or would have hired someone to kill him or would have pestered him into submission.

Typical feminist witchcraft stuff. He would have lost his wife, or more likely, he would have lost his life. He would have been killed like Naboth for not giving up his inheritance. "But Naboth said to Ahab, 'The Lord forbid that I should give the inheritance of my fathers to you!'" (1 Kings 21:3). Naboth said to Ahab what Ahab should have said to Jezebel. Ahab is given the vineyard of Israel to cultivate as an inheritance, but he gives it to Jezebel. Naboth refuses to give his vineyard to Jezebel and gets killed (1 Kings 21). Naboth did what Ahab should have done. Ahab coming to Naboth and offering him a better vineyard is like Satan offering Jesus a better vineyard in the desert. Jezebel's scheming to kill Naboth is like the scheming of the Pharisees to kill Jesus. Naboth represents what Ahab should have done, which was to sacrifice himself, as Christ did.

Additionally, if Ahab had taken down the idolatrous calf worship, the people may have revolted, or they may have decided to worship in Jerusalem, where they were supposed to, and their allegiance would have been more sympathetic to the rulers in Judah. He would have risked his place as ruler of Northern Israel.

These are the sins that Christian pastors are currently committing. Not every conservative pastor is committing these sins to the same degree, but many are committing them to some degree by facilitating the sin of Christians and being ruled by Jezebel, either literally by their wives or spiritually by the Jezebelian pressure to allow adulterous marriages to abide. This really is the sin of Adam. Ahab recommits the sin of Adam by being a weak man who is unwilling to enter into conflict and sacrifice himself, just like our ecclesiastical leadership.

Jezebel's sin is the sin of Eve. She dealt with the question "Did God really say?" a long time ago, and answered with a resounding "No, Baal is God." And then she proceeds to murderously insist that everyone worship the way she sees fit. She's not ashamed of her nakedness, which is her sin, but instead enlists her sin to manipulate and control and manufacture situations according to her will. In some ways, she's setting herself up as a god. Her witchcraft is a grasping at deity and sovereignty, which is what enticed Eve: "You will be like God" (Genesis 3:5). It is why Satan was thrown out of heaven, and it's what will keep you out of heaven. There's only one sovereign Lord, and it's God—not Satan, not Jezebel, and not you. Through the sin of Ahab and Jezebel, death is brought to the whole house of Ahab. Through the sin of Adam and Eve, death is brought to the whole human race.

This story is all history in miniature. The house of Ahab mocked and killed the servants and prophets of God, to its own destruction. This happened again to Jerusalem in 587 BC: "They mocked the messengers of God, and despised His words, and misused His prophets, until the wrath of the Lord arose against His people until there was no remedy" (2 Chronicles 36:14–16). It happened again in AD 70, after God's people mocked and killed the Prophet Jesus, the Messiah, the Anointed One. It's going to happen again at the end of history: "Because he hath appointed a day on which he will judge the world in righteousness by that man whom he has ordained" (Acts 17:31). Like Jehu, as a warrior-king appointed by God to judge the house of Ahab in righteousness, Jesus is our greater Warrior-King who will do the same to all who persist in sin without repentance and to all who refuse to submit to the lordship of Christ in all things—their end will be like Joram's, like Ahaziah's, and like Jezebel's.

Just as Jehu gives an opportunity for those in the house of Ahab to follow him, so does Jesus. Jehu says, "Turn around and follow me." And Jesus says the same. "Follow Me," Jesus says. "Pick up your cross. Follow Me. I'm calling on all men to repent. I'm executing judgment on the wicked. I'm putting all enemies and wicked rulers down and saving those who turn and follow Me." This is the good news. It is the gospel.

CHAPTER 8

BEAUTY WILL SAVE THE WORLD

THERE ARE MANY REASONS GOD made women beautiful. Among them is to teach us good eschatology. A beautiful and virtuous woman will attract the attention of men. Similarly, a beautiful and virtuous Church will attract men. They will be drawn to her beauty, just as the Lord Himself will be drawn to her: "I am my beloved's, and his desire is toward me" (Song of Songs 8:12). Her beauty will be her righteousness (Revelation 19:8). She will be the embodiment of the classical transcendentals, the good, the true, and the beautiful, just as Christ is. His wife, who is His own body, is being made into His likeness, as everything that is His is also hers. This reality obtains actual sanctification and deliverance from sin and her enemies. We are conforming more and more to His image. The more that image resembles Christ, the more the bride of Christ will be beautified and be attractive to the world, especially in contrast to an ugly and whorish secular, postmodern alternative.

But right now, the Church is not attractive, because she is as ugly and whorish as the world. Obviously, the conservative areas of the Church are more pure than the liberal areas, but the conservative branch of the Church is the gateway through which the demonic is being allowed to destroy the entire body. The conservative branch of the Church may not have lesbian bishops, but it opened the door to let them come in. This is why I have spoken so critically to the conservative leadership in this book. A little leaven leavens the whole lump, so don't be puffed up with pride and arrogance about how prosperous and orthodox your conservative denomination is. Your protection of that little bit of leaven has been the cause of immeasurable damage.

Covenant Blessings and Curses

The damage we have witnessed and are experiencing should come as no surprise. But the Christian world is surprised because it doesn't acknowledge that God interacts with the world on the basis of His covenant with men. Much of the evangelical world simply makes no connection between personal and cultural destruction, and the sin in their lives and in their churches. They just think they are righteous, like Job, and are experiencing similar loss, when in reality they are not blameless servants. They are guilty, as Ham, Achan, and Ahab were. When men are obedient to the law of God, blessings are manifest. When men are disobedient to the law, curses are. This type of covenantal thinking needs to feature much more prominently in our minds once again. It is important not only for the life of the individual but also for the life of the Church, and ultimately for the life of the world. Peter Lillback explains further:

> God's plans and promises in His covenant are not dependent upon man and are consequently unconditional. Nevertheless, at any given point in human history, God's blessings are to be responded to in human responsibility by obedience to the covenant. Without such obedience, the blessings of God shall be removed in divine judgment. From man's temporal standpoint, the covenant is conditional. From God's eternal perspective it is unconditional. God will never fail to keep His word, but if the covenant people fail to keep their word, they shall lose the covenant blessings.[67]

R. J. Rushdoony is also helpful on this point of covenantal conditionality:

> The word of God is a seamless garment, and men who deny its law deny its eschatology also, and are deprived of God's power. It is not surprising, therefore, that this is an era of impotence in the church. That impotence will no more be cured by frantic and earnest prayer meetings than was the problem of Baal's prophets by their shouts, "O Baal, hear us" (1 Kings 18:26). True faith means law-obedience, and obedience

---

67 Peter Lillback, *The Binding of God: Calvin's Role in the Development of Covenant Theology* (Grand Rapids: Baker Academic, 2001), 170.

spells power and blessing. Deuteronomy 28 tells us precisely, and for all time, how prayers are answered and a people blessed.[68]

Rushdoony is absolutely justified in taking a swipe at prayer meetings. He's exactly right. You can pray for reformation and revival as earnestly and frantically as you want, but as long as you continue to disobey the law of Christ (see Matthew 5:32, Matthew 19:9, Mark 10:11–12, Luke 16:18, 1 Corinthians 7:10–11, 7:39, and Romans 7:2–3) and disregard the call to repent of your adulterous marriages, the Church will continue to be powerless. Deuteronomy 28 does tell us how these prayers are answered and a people blessed. It's tempting to quote the entire chapter here, but I will highlight only a few portions.

While the curses and blessings have a primary application to the children of Israel according to the flesh, the curses and blessings have a fulfilled application to the true children of Israel, those who have faith in Christ, the Church. Paul says, "Understand, then, that those who have faith are children of Abraham" (Galatians 3:7). This means that, in one sense, some Israelites who physically descended from Abraham are not part of Israel: "For not all who are descended from Israel belong to Israel" (Romans 9:6). Conversely, some gentiles who did not physically descend from Abraham are part of Israel: "For neither circumcision counts for anything, nor uncircumcision, but a new creation. Peace and mercy to all who follow this rule—to the Israel of God" (Galatians 6:16). Everyone who places faith in Christ is a true Israelite. In short, the Church is Israel. The Church did not replace Israel. The Church *is* Israel and always has been.

Another way to think of this is that Abraham was a Christian. The gospel was preached to Abraham, and Abraham believed that gospel (Galatians 3:8). Everyone who believed, with Abraham, that the Seed of Abraham would bless the nations was also a Christian. So Moses was a Christian, David was a Christian, Elijah was a Christian, and so forth. While Israel according to the flesh is, in another sense, distinct from true Israel (Romans 11:28), just as Paul says, and this is a mystery (Romans 11:25), I am emphasizing the continuity

---

68 Rousas John Rushdoony, foreword to Greg Bahnsen's *Theonomy in Christian Ethics* (Nacogdoches: Covenant Media Press, 2002), xiii.

of who God's people are between the different covenants to show that the blessings and curses promised and threatened to Israel according to the flesh belong to true Israel, the Church.

I will cite one example from Paul that clearly demonstrates that this is the case, and then move on. When Paul is writing to the gentiles in Ephesus, he quotes Deuteronomy 5:16 to them and says that the obedience they render to the law will be rewarded with blessing: "Children, obey your parents in the Lord, for this is right. 'Honor your father and mother,' which is the first commandment with promise: 'that it may be well with you and you may live long on the earth'" (Ephesians 6:1–3). Here, Paul clearly applies the covenantal blessings—and by implication, curses—of Israel according to the flesh to the Church. Let me say this again. Paul applies Old Covenant promises to New Covenant people. The covenantal blessings and curses given to the nation of Israel are expanded and applied to Gentile converts. The covenant of God now invades the entire world. The blessing is expanded from the Promised Land in Palestine to the land outside of Palestine, to the whole earth. This is why I have treated the Church as recipients of the covenantal blessings and curses enumerated in the Old Covenant throughout this book.

What is incredible about the covenant is that the blessings and curses are manifest in history. They are not concerned merely with spiritual blessings and spiritual curses. "And all people of the earth shall see that thou art called by the name of the Lord; and they shall be afraid of thee" (Deuteronomy 28:10). As Gary DeMar notes of Deuteronomy 28:10, "The point here is: these blessings are not merely internal, 'spiritual-only' blessings; they are public blessings. They are blessings that differentiate covenant-keepers from covenant-breakers, not merely in eternity, but in time and on earth."[69] The blessings will be visible testimonies to the enemies of God. As you read through Deuteronomy 28 and other areas of promise and threat in Scripture, you begin to see an eerie correlation between what is described there and what we witness in history and what we are currently witnessing.

---

69 Publisher's preface to John Calvin's *The Covenant Enforced: Sermons on Deuteronomy 27 and 28* (Tyler: Institute for Christian Economics, 1990), xv.

The threat of curses is as follows: "But it shall come to pass, if you do not obey the voice of the Lord your God, to observe carefully all His commandments and His statutes which I command you today, that all these curses will come upon you and overtake you" (Deuteronomy 28:15).

Some of the curses that we see today are these:

The Church has been losing its authority and effectiveness in Western culture steadily for several decades. "The Lord will cause you to be defeated before your enemies; you shall go out one way against them and flee seven ways before them; and you shall become troublesome to all the kingdoms of the earth" (Deuteronomy 28:25).

The civil government, because we have made it our god, steals almost half of the fruits of our labor. It demands that we sacrifice approximately four times as much as the Lord requires of us. Much of this money goes to the enemies of God, people who hate us, through welfare, foreign aid, student loans, public schools, and so on. "Your ox shall be slaughtered before your eyes, but you shall not eat of it; your donkey shall be violently taken away from before you, and shall not be restored to you; your sheep shall be given to your enemies, and you shall have no one to rescue them" (Deuteronomy 28:31).

The children of many believing Christians, both spiritual children via conversion and physical children, apostatize because their parents have broken the covenant. Thus, God gives them over to other people. "Your sons and your daughters shall be given to another people, and your eyes shall look and fail with longing for them all day long; and there shall be no strength in your hand…you shall beget sons and daughters, but they shall not be yours; for they shall go into captivity" (Deuteronomy 28:32, 28:41).

America is being overrun by illegal immigrants. Europe is being taken over by Muslims. Both are draining the resources of the countries. Illegal immigrants in America benefit from our numerous entitlement programs (as do lazy Americans). Muslims in Europe are literally being given vacation homes of native Europeans and numerous other entitlements as well. These immigrants, particularly the Muslims, have little interest in assimilation. They are aware that the world is religious, and they are intent on overthrowing the Christian West. "A nation whom you have not known shall eat the fruit of your land and the produce of your labor, and you shall be only oppressed and crushed continually. So you shall be driven mad because of the sight which your eyes see…the alien who is among you shall rise higher and higher above you, and you shall come down lower and lower. He shall lend to you, but you shall not lend to him; he shall be the head, and you shall be the tail" (Deuteronomy 28:33–34, 28:43–44). The lending clause is interesting too, as we owe other countries, such as China, enormous amounts of money.

All our preaching of the gospel, evangelism, church building, and attempts at reclaiming the culture are yielding less and less fruit. "You shall carry much seed out to the field but gather little in, for the locust shall consume it. You shall plant vineyards and tend them, but you shall neither drink of the wine nor gather the grapes; for the worms shall eat them" (Deuteronomy 28:38–39).

Christian men and women who would otherwise be quite-pleasant people deal treacherously with one another. "The sensitive and very refined man among you will be hostile toward his brother, toward the wife of his bosom, and toward the rest of his children whom he leaves behind…the tender and delicate woman among you, who would not venture to set the sole of her foot on the ground because of her delicateness and sensitivity, her eye shall be evil toward the husband of her bosom, and to her son and her daughter" (Deuteronomy 28:54–56). This curse culminated in literal cannibalism, which we have not seen, but Paul compares not loving your neighbor as yourself to cannibalism, which is indeed what we are witnessing (Galatians 5:14–15).

These curses were manifested in the cycles of disobedience in the times of the judges and kings and were ultimately fulfilled in the Babylonian captivity of Israel, but as I argued above, I believe they can be properly applied to the Church, and we can learn from the general equity being taught here, the principles derived from these passages. We can also learn from the historical record of the Church in her infancy. When she was disobedient, these curses would come on her. She would be given over to her enemies and, ultimately, given over to the Babylonians. But we can learn from these things and apply what we learn to the Church, which ought to know better, as she is no longer in her infancy: "Now these things happened as examples for us, so that we would not crave evil things as they also craved" (1 Corinthians 10:6). Not only can we learn not to make the same mistakes as they did, but we can be encouraged and take hope: "For whatever things were written before were written for our learning, that we through the patience and comfort of the Scriptures might have hope" (Romans 15:4).

Just as Israel's disobedience manifested in curses, so too did its obedience manifest in blessings. As we surveyed in this book, Joshua's and Gideon's victories in battle were preceded by fidelity to the covenant. God blessed the kings of Israel proportionately to their degree of faithfulness to the covenant. And the law itself testifies to these realities.

> Then it shall come to pass, because you listen to these judgments, and keep and do them, that the Lord your God will keep with you the covenant and the mercy which He swore to your fathers. And He will love you and bless you and multiply you; He will also bless the fruit of your womb and the fruit of your land, your grain and your new wine and your oil, the increase of your cattle and the offspring of your flock, in the land of which He swore to your fathers to give you. You shall be blessed above all peoples; there shall not be a male or female barren among you or among your livestock. And the Lord will take away from you all sickness, and will afflict you with none of the terrible diseases of Egypt which you have known, but will lay them on all those who hate you. Also you shall destroy all the peoples whom the Lord your God delivers over to you; your eye shall have no pity on them; nor shall you serve their gods, for that will be a snare to you. (Deuteronomy 7:12–16)
>
> None shall miscarry or be barren in your land; I will fulfill the number of your days. (Exodus 23:26)

These promises are given to us on the condition that we listen to, keep, and do the commandments of the Lord. We are promised fruitfulness in every area of life. We are promised that Christians will not be barren or afflicted with sickness or terrible disease. God will fulfill the number of our days. Isaiah affirms this when prophesying concerning the new heavens and new earth, which we are currently living in: "Never again will there be in it an infant who lives but a few days, or an old man who does not live out his years; the one who dies at a hundred will be thought a mere child; the one who fails to reach a hundred will be considered accursed" (Isaiah 65:20). Notice that in the new heavens and the new earth, people still die, but their lives are extended. I believe the Lord began creating the new heavens and the new earth during His earthly ministry and they have been manifesting ever since, like leaven in bread or a seed that grows to be a tree (Matthew 13:31–33). Of course, in the fullest manifestation of the new heavens and new earth we will have our resurrected and glorified bodies and will reign with Christ for eternity. But for now we inhabit the growing manifestation of God's will in heaven being realized here on earth, just as our Lord taught us to pray. And He wouldn't teach us to pray this if it wasn't going to happen would He?

In the new heavens and new earth, there still exists blessings and cursings according to the covenant. Participating in the New Covenant sacrament in an unworthy manner can bring sickness and death: "For he who eats and drinks in an unworthy manner eats and drinks judgment to himself, not discerning the Lord's body. For this reason many are weak and sick among you, and many sleep" (1 Corinthians 11:29–30). But if participation in the New Covenant is done in a worthy manner, then you are blessed: "Is not the cup of blessing which we bless a sharing in the blood of Christ? Is not the bread which we break a sharing in the body of Christ?" (1 Corinthians 10:16). The New Covenant is a cup of blessing when taken in a worthy manner, when lived in obedience and in submission to the law of Christ.

We are promised economic prosperity and dominance over other nations: "The Lord will open to you His good treasure, the heavens, to give the rain to your land in its season, and to bless all the work of your hand. You shall lend to many nations, but you shall not borrow. And the Lord will make you the head and not the tail; you shall be above only, and not be beneath, if you heed the commandments of the Lord your God, which I command you today, and are careful to observe them" (Deuteronomy 28:12–13).

We are promised the kings of the nations: "He will deliver their kings into your hand, and you will destroy their name from under heaven; no one shall be able to stand against you until you have destroyed them" (Deuteronomy 28:24). I believe this means the conversion of entire nations, including their political regimes and national treasures (scientific advancements, artistic achievements, natural resources, etc.). We see this prophesied in Isaiah— "Nations will come to your light, and kings to the brightness of your rising" (Isaiah 60:30)—and in Haggai—"'I will shake all the nations; and they will come with the wealth of all nations, and I will fill this house with glory,' says the Lord of hosts" (Haggai 2:17). This is typified in King Solomon's rule: "So King Solomon surpassed all the kings of the earth in riches and wisdom. And all the kings of the earth sought the presence of Solomon to hear his wisdom, which God had put in his heart. Each man brought his present: articles of silver and gold, garments, armor, spices, horses, and mules, at a set rate year by year" (2 Chronicles 9:22–24). Christ, who is the greater Solomon, is greater than all the kings of the earth. He is the king of all other kings. And the temple of the Lord is His people, the Church. Their obedience to His covenant results in the nations being drawn to the Church and bringing their treasures and the kingdom of God establishing itself on earth as it is in heaven. After all, this is how Jesus teaches us to pray (Matthew 6:10).

Greater Glory

If obedience to God's commands manifests itself in blessings and cultural dominance, then the Church is being disobedient somewhere. The area of disobedience is divorce and remarriage. Jesus taught us to follow the ancient path as modeled in the Garden of Eden, but we have rejected it: "Thus says the LORD, 'Stand by the ways and see and ask for the ancient paths, Where the good way is, and walk in it; and you will find rest for your souls.' But they said, 'We will not walk in it'" (Jeremiah 6:16). Other explanations for the waning power of the Church point to either symptoms or things that are not as significant. Alternative explanations are simply unconvincing to me. Some conservative leaders in the Church give lip service to the problem of divorce and remarriage but certainly not nearly to the same extent as they do to symptoms such as homosexuality or abortion or any number of other cultural issues that are certainly sinful but are more difficult to prove as being sinful from Scripture than divorce and remarriage.

There are plenty of capable pastors and theologians who see that something is wrong and have given their thoughts on why.[70] But these attempts consistently misdiagnose the problem. They address only symptoms. For example, Douglas Wilson says, "The reformation of the family is at the heart of the reformation of the Church...in a godly culture, the first social manifestation of grace is found in the family. But our culture is so rebellious that we have institutionalized our rebellion and cannot even conceive of how a genuine obedience would appear."[71] Pastor Wilson correctly teaches that the family needs to be reformed first in order to reform the Church and that grace in the family will manifest grace elsewhere. Three cheers to this! But he then describes the culture as institutionalizing our rebellion, which does not adequately describe our situation. The culture is simply mimicking the institutionalized rebellion of the Church. And *it is the Church* that cannot even conceive of how genuine obedience would appear.

The Church is obedient in many areas and has advanced from glory to glory over the past ten thousand years. We have much to be enthusiastically thankful for. Most first world nations have a strong Protestant heritage. Most second world nations have either a Roman Catholic or an Eastern Orthodox heritage. And most third world nations are still pagan. The blessings we have received are directly related to the Church's obedience of the covenant and her faithfulness in discipleship of the nations.

The last five hundred years have been a reaping of the harvest sowed by the Protestant Reformation, for better and for worse. The return to the supreme authority of God's word over all life, the desire for pure religion, the ability for all men to have access to Scripture in their own language, and many more things are some of the treasures recovered at the Reformation. And some of us simply take for granted and fail to give thanks for these things and only complain about the faults and flaws of the Reformation, while others are too

---

70 Douglas Wilson, *Mother Kirk: Essays on Church Life* (Moscow: Canon Press, 2001), 15.

71 Ibid, 17.

infatuated with the Reformation to even see the flaws. America is the greatest nation that has ever existed in the history of the world, and I believe the Reformation was one of the many reasons for this. "Righteousness exalts a nation, but sin is a reproach to any people" (Proverbs 14:34). The Reformation recovered many sound doctrines and revived the holiness of God's people, who eventually made a home in America.

While the Reformation had its own glory, we must realize that we are still advancing in glory to greater glory. The Reformation was not perfect. It had its defects. "Respect for the Reformation as a divine work in no way forbids the admission that it included some mixture of error and sin; as where God builds a church, the devil erects a chapel by its side."[72] And as I have argued in this book, the inchoate chapel that the devil began erecting at the Reformation was the doctrine of adulterous marriage. The fundamental hurdle to advancing in greater glory is our acceptance of covenant breaking in divorce and remarriage. This was an enemy that was not destroyed in the war of the Reformation. "The Lord your God will drive out those nations before you little by little; you will be unable to destroy them at once, lest the beasts of the field become too numerous for you" (Deuteronomy 7:22).

The advancement of the kingdom is progressive, and our enemies are not taken out all at once. I believe this can be understood in terms of doctrinal purity as well. God has determined to unfold history this way so that we will be able to master the land, enemies, and doctrine we have conquered; otherwise we would be overwhelmed by the beasts of the field (whatever they may be: our pride, tribalism, complacency, presumptuousness, etc.). Also, God does not totally eradicate our enemies or give us 100 percent pure doctrine from former battles, because He wants our children to know war: "Now these are the nations which the Lord left, that He might test Israel by them, that is, all who had not known any of the wars in Canaan. This was only so that the generations of the children of Israel might be taught to know war, at least those who had not formerly known it" (Judges 3:1–2). God kept some of the

---

72 Philip Schaff, *The Principle of Protestantism* (Eugene: Wipf and Stock Publishers, 1845), 225.

tribes from being destroyed so that the children of the warriors would also become warriors.

God did this during the Protestant Reformation, but many of the children of the warriors of the Reformation refuse to go to war against the real enemies of our time. They are busy tilting at windmills. They are busy running about with fire extinguishers wherever there is a flood (to borrow a phrase from Lewis). They are busy arguing about common grace or forms of liturgical worship, or if they are feeling really bold, they might even take a stand against homosexuality. These children of the Reformation are busy being paintball warriors. They don't know the misery of true war, and they don't understand who the enemy is. They're tourists on a battlefield. They're arsonists who volunteer at the fire department. It's good to put out fires, but they're the ones starting them. They don't understand what the Spirit of the Lord is speaking to the churches. But they are part of the body of Christ, and we need them, just as they need us. There is not one part of the body that we don't need and that the Lord does not cherish. And in this hour, we need the body to be unified in her warfare.

Men, you are made for greatness. I see your desire to fight. I see your desire to win battles for the kingdom. I see that you have talents and skills and strengths that exponentially exceed my own and many in my tribe. The weapons you could bring to the fight are powerful. I am asking you to be great, to gain a better a resurrection, to desire glory, to sacrifice yourself for the cause of the kingdom, to fight the real battle.

A teacher of mine once pointed out that if you look at the world in five-hundred-year chunks, you can observe the steady progress of the kingdom of God in the world. It's chaotic, and it goes up and down. It goes five steps forward and two steps back. It treks through peaks and valleys, but it's ultimately ascending a mountain.

I believe it's significant that we are now approaching the five-hundredth anniversary of the Protestant Reformation. I believe we are on the precipice of another reformation. There are two aspects that I believe will be present in this reformation. I believe it will be a refinement and assimilation of the Pentecostal movement into every area of the Church. I have not mentioned this aspect in this book, because that is not its focus, but I believe it is important to mention because the Holy Spirit's gifts are necessary for the kind of warfare we will be entering into. I do not have time to elaborate on this now, but life in the Spirit is not to be despised, just as intelligence reports and heavy machine guns are not to be despised if you want to win wars.

The other aspect, the fundamental aspect of this coming reformation, will be repentance from adulterous marriages. It is going to look something like Ezra 9–10. Our situation and the coming reformation are not and will not be identical in every aspect to the situation and reformation found in Ezra 9–10, but they are similar.

In Ezra 9–10, the Israelites had entered into unlawful marriages and, in their repentance, divorced all their unlawful wives. "Then Ezra the priest stood up and said to them, 'You have transgressed and have taken pagan wives, adding to the guilt of Israel. Now therefore, make confession to the Lord God of your fathers, and do His will; separate yourselves from the peoples of the land, and from the pagan wives'" (Ezra 10:10–11). We are not to divorce pagan spouses in the New Covenant era if we become Christian while married to pagans, but we are to divorce spouses of unlawful marriages, just as the Israelites did here. The law of Christ forbids the taking of a divorced person, and so it logically follows that we are to divorce a spouse taken unlawfully.

Also of note is the level of astonishment and severe chastisement by Nehemiah and Ezra: "I rebuked them and called curses down on them. I beat some of the men and pulled out their hair. I made them take an oath in God's name and said: 'You are not to give your daughters in marriage to their sons, nor are you to take their daughters in marriage for your sons or for yourselves'" (Nehemiah 13:25).

So when I heard this thing, I tore my garment and my robe, and plucked out some of the hair of my head and beard, and sat down astonished. Then everyone who trembled at the words of the God of Israel assembled to me, because of the transgression of those who had been carried away captive, and I sat astonished until the evening sacrifice. At the evening sacrifice I arose from my fasting; and having torn my garment and my robe, I fell on my knees and spread out my hands to the Lord my God. And I said: "O my God, I am too ashamed and humiliated to lift up my face to You, my God; for our iniquities have risen higher than our heads, and our guilt has grown up to the heavens. Since the days of our fathers to this day we have been very guilty, and for our iniquities we, our kings, and our priests have been delivered into the hand of the kings of the lands, to the sword, to captivity, to plunder, and to humiliation, as it is this day. And now for a little while grace has been shown from the Lord our God, to leave us a remnant to escape, and to give us a peg in His holy place, that our God may enlighten our eyes and give us a measure of revival in our bondage. For we were slaves. Yet our God did not forsake us in our bondage; but He extended mercy to us in the sight of the kings of Persia, to revive us, to repair the house of our God, to rebuild its ruins, and to give us a wall in Judah and Jerusalem." (Ezra 9:3–9)

I hope that the Lord extends mercy to us. I believe He will and already has. As mentioned in an earlier chapter, when we pray for reformation, we are praying for a glorious, spectacular mess. We are praying for something that will fill us with consternation when we begin to see it. But that consternation will be eclipsed by the glory of its bounty. We will enter closer to that time when "the earth will be filled with the knowledge of the glory of the Lord, as the waters cover the sea" (Habakkuk 2:14). We will have defeated another enemy and discarded its carcass on the pile of dead bodies that have opposed themselves against the Christ: "For He must reign till He has put all enemies under His feet. The last enemy that will be destroyed is death" (1 Corinthians 15:25–26).

We will be that much closer to Christ, returning and destroying death. We will enter into yet another stage of glory in the new heavens and new earth. History began in a garden paradise, and it is moving toward a greater paradise, a garden city, the New Jerusalem. History began with a marriage, and it will end with a marriage.

When God created the world, He spoke light out of darkness. His first act of creation involved bringing forth light. The speaking of God's word brings light to dark places, and it creates new worlds. When Christ came and brought His kingdom, He began creating a new world and destroying the old one. He inaugurated the beginning of a new creation, a new heavens, and a new earth. The proclamation and practice of the gospel is what it means to participate in God's creation of the new heavens and the new earth. It is still being created, and we are able to participate in that glorious process. But being part of that process involves sacrificing yourself, picking up your cross, and giving your life for the sake of others and for the sake of the kingdom.

I love my God, and I love His people. I pray that you have been encouraged and emboldened by this book. I hope that those of you who were looking for answers found some. I hope that those of you who were considering divorcing your spouses are now reevaluating that decision. I hope that those of you who are Christians and are in adulterous marriages will repent by separating yourselves from your unlawful situations and remain single. Some people are made eunuchs for the sake of the kingdom. I hope that those of you who are divorced are now willing to remain single or be reconciled and that those of you who were interested in marrying a divorced person no longer are. I hope that those of you who are single and looking to get married now see more clearly the seriousness of the marriage covenant. I hope that those of you who have been ordained to shepherd God's flock will repent of causing these little ones to stumble and that you will be courageous enough to sacrifice everything for the sake of preaching the full truth of Christ's gospel.

We need you to be strong. We need you to be courageous. Lead us by your example. Fight for us. "Have I not commanded you? Be strong and courageous. Do not be afraid; do not be discouraged, for the Lord your God will be with you wherever you go" (Joshua 1:9).

www.ingramcontent.com/pod-product-compliance
Lightning Source LLC
Chambersburg PA
CBHW072009040426
42447CB00009B/1556